The Guises of
The Morrígan

*The Irish Goddess of Sex and Battle
Her Myths, Powers and Mysteries*

David Rankine & Sorita D'Este

Published by Avalonia

BM Avalonia
London
WC1N 3XX
England, UK

www.avaloniabooks.co.uk

First Edition 2005
Copyright © David Rankine and Sorita D'Este

Illustrations by Brian Andrews
Design by Avalonia

ISBN 1-905297-00-9

A CIP catalogue record for this volume is available from the
British Library and the US Library of Congress on request.

Dedication

This book is dedicated to our corvid friend
who shared our house "that" spring and taught us
the secret mysteries of the Crow.

Acknowledgements

Thank you to everyone who has helped and supported us towards the
completion of this project - Phil & Tracy of Stagman Creations, Prof.
Ronald Hutton, Brian Andrews, Ian Foot, Harry Greenfield & the
friendly staff at the British Library. Also a big thank you to all the
beautiful members of Vitriol Grove who have had to listen to our
frequent diatribes about this project for quite some time!

Contents

Introduction

The Morrígan is probably the most powerful yet mysterious figure amongst the Celtic Gods. The popular image of the Morrígan is as the Goddess of Battle and Sex, a perception that only scratches the surface of this complex and manifold Goddess.

From Bestower of Sovereignty to Earth Goddess, from Lady of the Beasts to Faery Queen, from Lover to Witch Goddess, the Morrígan stands out as one of the pre-eminent Celtic Goddesses. More than any other Celtic deity the Morrígan embodies the resurgence of the divine feminine, appearing in a wide variety of guises to express the full spectrum of feminine power.

The strength and control the Morrígan displays, as well as her ferocity and tenacity, and her ability to control events to ensure the desired result are all displayed repeatedly in the myths. As a Liminal Goddess the Morrígan connects not only the different realms of earth, sky, sea and otherworld, but also the myths of the British Isles through her different guises.

The major references to the Morrígan working with the other gods occur in the battle between the Túatha Dé Danann and the Fir Bolgs (*The First Battle of Moytura*), and the later battle between the Túatha Dé Danann and the Fomorians (*The Second Battle of Moytura*). In the former she acts as both magician and warrior, and in the latter her roles as Battle Goddess and Prophetess are given more emphasis.

As the tutelary Goddess of the hero Cú Chulainn she displays a number of her qualities and roles. Her role as instigator of conflict is emphasised, by stealing the cow which precipitates the events leading to all the conflicts described in the Táin (*Táin Bó Cúailnge*). The Morrígan appears in a wide range of forms during this tale, as a maiden and a crone, as a crow, and in the eel, wolf and cow forms which she uses to attack Cú Chulainn.

As well as her shape-shifting ability, the Morrígan again uses her power to prophesy, both as a crow and as the Washer at the Ford when she foretells the hero's death. She also uses spells and enchantments to achieve her desired results, and her terrible shriek to kill Cú Chulainn's enemies.

By considering the different versions of the Celtic myths and legends together, the number of guises the Morrígan assumes becomes much more evident than has previously been credited. This includes her links to other Goddesses, like the Welsh Rhiannon, Don and Modron; the Irish Boand, Danu, Ériu, Fea and Grian; the British Goddess Andraste, and the Gallic Goddesses Epona and Nantosuelta.

The different guises she assumes in the tale of Cú Chulainn are also more numerous than has been previously credited. By exploring the symbols and roles of the female figures within this myth it becomes clear that the warrior women Búannan and Scáthach, the warrior queen Medb and the prophetess Fedelm are all guises of the Morrígan.

In other tales the Morrígan appears in a whole range of guises. She is the Cailleach (crone) who bestows sovereignty on a worthy king, or takes it from an unworthy one. As the Faery Queen we see a whole range of faery beings across the British Isles and France deriving their qualities and appearance from her.

The Morrígan also assumed a number of guises in literature. The best known of these is probably as Morgan Le Fay in the Arthurian cycle of stories. However as the Faery Queen she also inspired many poets and writers throughout the centuries, from William Shakespeare to W.B. Yeats. Her effect on the literature of the last thousand years is explored through reference to the breadth of her influence.

This book, which is the result of many years of research and exploration of the myths, mysteries and guises of the Morrígan, makes available for the first time in one place a body of material which demonstrates the full extent of her importance from the ancient Celtic world through to modern times.

It is our hope that through this work the reader will come to a greater appreciation of the many and diverse guises of the Morrígan.

David Rankine & Sorita D'Este
March 2005

1. The Morrígan in Celtic Mythology

Through the Irish myths the Morrígan is usually found whenever there is a major conflict. Hence we first see her appearing during the invasion of Ireland by the Túatha Dé Danann[1], a race of Gods who are looking for a new land to colonise. The Túatha Dé Danann arrived in Ireland in their fleet of ships with a whole host of accompanying heroes and followers.

The Fir Bolgs, who were the indigenous Gods already living in Ireland, were not keen to share their land. The Túatha Dé Danann sent out Bres, one of their heroes, to scout the land. Bres met a Fir Bolg hero called Sreng. The two talked, and Bres relayed to Sreng the message that the Túatha Dé Danann had declared that they would be happy to live in peace providing the Fir Bolgs give them half of Ireland.

The descriptions of the Túatha Dé Danann present them as clean-limbed and beautiful, in contrast to the misshapen and monstrous Fir Bolgs. This story represents the theme of a new lawful order replacing an older and more chaotic, primal order. The same theme is found in the Greek myths, where the Olympian pantheon overthrew the earlier and more primal Titan Gods to become the ruling power.

After defeating the Fir Bolgs and allowing them a small part of Ireland to live in, the Túatha Dé Danann settled in as the new ruling power. However they were soon being attacked by the Fomorians, a pirate race who demanded tribute or threatened invasion if they were not paid off. The Fomorians were also described as being monstrous and so clearly represent another manifestation of the earlier and more chaotic order.

After a number of years of paying tribute, the Túatha Dé Danann decided to go to war with the Fomorians, and stop paying the tribute. The Fomorians launched an invasion force, and a fierce battle was fought for control of Ireland. With the aid of the Morrígan the Túatha Dé Danann were victorious and permanently destroyed the Fomorian threat.

---

[1] Children of Dana or Danu. They are also sometimes referred to as the *"Men of Dea"*. Confusingly this term was initially used to describe not just the Gods but also the human followers.

Subsequent Irish myths are more concerned with the actions of heroes, some of whom are semi-divine. These heroes are the result of unions between members of the Túatha Dé Danann and humans. However the Morrígan still plays a role in many of these hero myths, especially those featuring the greatest Irish hero, Cú Chulainn.

We will consider these two sets of divine conflicts and the tales of Cú Chulainn to show how significant a role the Morrígan plays in the major Irish myths.

The War with the Fir Bolgs

The first attack in the conflict against the Fir Bolgs is carried out by the Morrígan with Badb and Macha. The Fir Bolgs are camped at Tara hill and the Túatha Dé Danann need to keep them there while they move to better ground, so they will have the advantage in the coming battle.

Morrígan, Badb and Macha work their magic, and are described as *"bringing down enchanted showers of sorcery and mighty showers of fire, and a downpour of red blood upon the warrior's heads, preventing them from moving for three days and nights."*[2]

At the gathering of the Gods and heroes of the Túatha Dé Danann before the battle, each God and hero in turn boasts of how brave they will be in the fight. After hearing this, the Goddess also states her intention to fight: *"We will go with you, said the women, that is, Badb, Macha, Morrígan and Danu."*[3]

Before the two sides engage in battle the Morrígan cries out: *"The badba and monsters and hags of doom cried out so that they were heard from the cliffs and waterfalls and in the hollows of the earth."*[4]

The Morrígan in several of her guises now sets a clear boundary for the battle, which makes it clear to the forces of the Túatha Dé Danann that there will be no retreat from the battlefield.

"The three sorceresses, Badb, Macha and Morrígan; Bé Chuille and Danu, their two foster-mothers. They fixed their pillars in the ground lest anyone flee before the stones should flee."[5]

The Túatha Dé Danann defeat the Fir Bolgs in the battle and take over Ireland. However during this combat the Túatha Dé Danann king, Nuada, loses his hand, and has to give up his rule. One of the laws of the Túatha Dé Danann was that to rule a God (or man) must be whole of body. He was replaced as king by Bres, a youth who is half Túatha Dé Danann and half Fomorian.

---

[2] *Cath Muighe Tuireadh (The First Battle of Moytura).*
[3] *Cath Muighe Tuireadh.*
[4] *Cath Muighe Tuireadh.*
[5] *Cath Muighe Tuireadh.*

Enchanted Showers of Sorcery

The War with the Fomorians

Subsequently the piratical and chaotic Fomorians started exacting tribute from the Túatha Dé Danann, and some years later a second war followed, which is recounted in the *Second Battle of Moytura*.[6]

The first influence of the Morrígan in the tale is subtle, for it is she who encourages the hero God Lugh to action: *"Then she said to him, 'Undertake a battle of overthrowing.' The Morrígan said to Lugh, 'Awake'."* [7]

Lugh is the key warrior in the Túatha Dé Danann army. He is the grandson of the Fomorian King and God Balor, whose eye kills any being he looks at. A prophecy has predicted that Lugh will kill Balor, so he needs to be present for the Túatha Dé Danann to win.

Lugh is equipped with special weapons made for him by the "three Gods of Danu", Brian, Luchar and Lucharba, who are named elsewhere as sons of the Morrígan.

The Túatha Dé Danann gather their forces and then send the Daghda out scouting to see what he can discover. He finds the Morrígan washing clothes at a ford, where she appears as a striking woman with nine red tresses in her hair.

They make love astride the ford, the Morrígan having one foot on each bank of the river. Afterwards the Morrígan tells the Daghda that the Fomorians will land at Mag Ceidne, and that he should summon all his champions to meet her at the Ford of Unshin.

She declares that she will destroy the Fomorian leader Indech, taking his heart's blood and testicles. After doing this she will gives two handfuls of blood to the warriors in blessing. As Indech turns up in the battle and is killed there, this seems to be a declaration of her intent to fight with the Túatha Dé Danann, rather than a pre-emptive action.

The Daghda continues scouting and finds the Fomorian army exactly where the Morrígan told him they would be. The Fomorians attempt to make him insult them, by offering him a huge pit full of porridge to eat. If he gives insult to the Fomorians it would give them ground to

---

[6] *Cath Maige Tuired (The Second Battle of Moytura).*
[7] *Cath Maige Tuired.*

kill him, but if he avoids insulting them they cannot harm him due to the laws of hospitality. The Daghda eats all the porridge, scraping it dry and then leaves after joking about the food.

On his way back to the Túatha Dé Danann army, the Daghda is accosted by a woman, who insults him, mocking his huge distended belly (from eating all the porridge). This woman is the daughter of the Fomorian king Indech, described in some sources as Boand, another guise of the Morrígan.

Subsequently the Daghda also has sex with her, and she offers her support to the Túatha Dé Danann, saying she will provide information on the Fomorian forces and act against them.

"She said that she would hinder the Fomorians, and she would sing spells against them ... and she alone would take on a ninth part of the host."[8]

After the Daghda has rejoined the Túatha Dé Danann army, the Gods and heroes indulge in the standard practice of boasting what they will do in the forthcoming battle.

When asked of her powers the Morrígan says: *"Not hard to say, I stand fast. I shall pursue whatever I watch. I shall destroy those I have my eye on."*[9]

The two sides engage in battle, and the sides are evenly matched. However after a while the Túatha Dé Danann started to waver. The Fomorians are not even deterred by the loss of their greatest fighter Balor, killed by Lugh. Then the Morrígan goes into the ranks of the Túatha Dé Danann with grim words, stiffening the hearts of the Túatha Dé Danann to fight fiercely and resolutely. In a short time the armies break apart, and the Fomorians are driven to the sea.

---

[8] *Cath Maige Tuired.*
[9] *Cath Maige Tuired.*

15

The Victory Prophecy

Following the battle, the Morrigan delivers a victory prophecy. This has two parts, the first of which is positive and indicates a period of prosperity, and the second of which is apocalyptic and predicts the end of the world.

"After the battle and the cleansing of the slaughter, Morrígan proclaimed the triumph and the great victory to the royal hills of Ireland, to its spirit army, to its waters and rivers and estuaries. And Badb, the sister of Morrígan prophesied:

> *'Peace to the sky, sky to the earth,*
> *earth beneath sky, strength in each;*
> *a cup very full, full of honey,*
> *honour enough, summer in winter;*
> *spear supported by shield,*
> *shields supported by forts,*
> *forts fierce eager for battle,*
> *fleece from sheep, woods full of stags,*
> *forever destructions have departed,*
> *mast on trees, a branch drooping-down,*
> *drooping from growth*
> *wealth for a son, a son very learned*
> *neck of bull in yoke, a bull from a song*
> *knots in woods, wood for a fire*
> *fire as wanted*
> *palisades new and bright*
> *salmon their victory, the Boyne their hostel*
> *hostel with an excellence of size*
> *new growth after spring*
> *in autumn horses increase*
> *the land held secure*
> *land recounted with excellence of word*
> *Be might to the eternal much excellent woods*
> *peace to sky be this nine times eternal.'*

However this was only half of the tale. For she also prophesied the end of the world, and she sang:

> *'I shall not see a world that will be dear to me.*
> *Summer without flowers, cows without milk,*
> *Women without modesty, men not brave,*

16

Conquests without a king.
Woods without mast, fishless seas,
Bad judgments by old men,
False precedents of the lawgivers.
Every man a betrayer, each son a robber,
The son will enter his father's bed
The father also in the bed of the son,
A brother becomes his own brother-in-law!
None will look for a woman outside his own house.
O evil time, deception, deception."[10]

The list of places where the triumph is proclaimed also gives a number of the qualities associated with the Morrígan. The reference to the *"royal hills of Ireland"* is a clear reference to her role as Bestower of Sovereignty. The *"spirit army"* implies her role as Faery or Phantom Queen (one of the translations of her name). The mention of *"its waters and rivers and estuaries"* emphasises flowing waters, associated with the Otherworld, and also her guise as a River Goddess.

---

[10] *Cath Maige Tuired.*

Encounters with Cú Chulainn

The Morrígan also plays an important role in the tales of Cú Chulainn (*"the Hound of Chulainn"*), acting as a tutelary Goddess to him, and turning up at most of the critical occasions in his life.

The love hate relationship between the two of them echoes the relationship between the war Goddess Ishtar and the hero Gilgamesh in the *Epic of Gilgamesh*, a Sumerian myth that is over 5,000 years old. In this myth Gilgamesh receives help from Ishtar when he does her bidding, but when he goes against her, or refuses her sexual advances, he experiences all sorts of problems and losses.

The link between the two is recognised by others, such as his compatriot Fer Diad, who trained with him under the mysterious warrior woman Scáthach, and who encourages his charioteer to take him to fight Cú Chulainn, saying: *"Let us go to this encounter to contend with this man [Cú Chulainn], until we reach the ford above which the Badb will shriek."*[11]

Badb's Mockery

The Morrígan first appears in Cú Chulainn's life when he is young. He wakes from sleep and goes outside to find his druid mentor Conchobar. Instead he encounters a phantom[12] with half a head, carrying a corpse on his back. The phantom throws the corpse at Cú Chulainn and demands that he carry it.

Cú Chulainn refuses and wrestles the phantom, which throws him to the ground. Badb appears and mocks him, causing Cú Chulainn to rise in fury and knocks the head off the phantom with his hurley stick.[13] The precocious young Cú Chulainn uses the phantom's head as a hurley ball whilst he continues looking for Conchobar.[14]

---

[11] *Táin Bó Cúailnge.*
[12] It is significant to remember that one translation of her name is *"Phantom Queen"*.
[13] A hurley stick is similar to a hockey stick, and is used in the old Irish sport of Hurling, which is still played today in a more regulated manner.
[14] A similar story occurs in the Icelandic *Grettir's Saga*, with the hero encountering a strong phantom that he beheads after wrestling.

After much searching Cú Chulainn is then able to find and rescue the King and his son from amidst the corpses of the battlefield, demonstrating his heroic nature.

Although at first glance this might not appear very helpful, inciting warriors to action by insult and ridicule, or *gressacht*, was a common practice amongst the Celts.

As he reaches maturity Cú Chulainn decides he needs a suitable wife. None of the women he considers match his standards until he remembers a beautiful and clever maiden called Emer. He courts her, but her father Forgall Monach is against the match.

Forgall approaches Cú Chulainn in disguise and tells him about the mysterious island of the warrior woman Scáthach. He entices Cú Chulainn by telling him that Scáthach trains the best warriors in the world. Although Forgall hopes that Cú Chulainn will die on the perilous journey to Scáthach's island, Cú Chulainn sees the journey and training as a chance to gain greater glory.

Scáthach

The island of Scáthach can only be reached by a bridge known as *Droichet na ndaltae* (the Bridge of the Fosterling), and then a series of tests must be undertaken for the candidate to prove his worthiness to be trained. Scáthach sends her daughter Úathach (whose name means *spectre*) to feed him, and Cú Chulainn responds by breaking her finger. When a man comes to her aid he kills him.

After three days Úathach tells him the three demands he must make of Scáthach in order to study with her. She must teach him without neglect, foretell his future, and allow him to marry Úathach without wedding gifts. When he meets Scáthach he puts his sword between her breasts and makes these demands, which she agrees to.

During his time being trained by Scáthach, Cú Chulainn fights another warrior woman called Aífe, who is Scáthach's enemy.[15] He defeats her and makes three demands of her: that she gives hostages to

---

[15] Some sources claim that Aífe is Scáthach's twin sister, and that they are both daughters of the Morrígan, e.g. *Chronicles of the Celts –* Peter Berresford Ellis.

Scáthach, that she spend the night with him, and that she bears him a son. She agrees and does all three.

Scáthach then teaches Cú Chulainn the arts of the warrior, including the mighty salmon leap, and the use of the deadly gae bolga spear, which is thrown with the feet. There is a bitter irony in the fact that two of the times he does use the Gae Bolga it is to kill his best friend and his son in combat.

It is interesting also to consider that the spear is associated with his father Lugh, so the blessing and acknowledgement of his divine father may also be implied by his gaining the spear, as he is the only warrior that Scáthach ever teaches to use the gae bolga.

After he returns from his training with Scáthach, Cú Chulainn continues to woo the maiden Emer, and wins her hand in marriage.[16] After this he encounters the Morrígan again. There are two completely different stories of this meeting, told in different versions of the Cú Chulainn myth.

The Morrígan's Offer

The first meeting between the Morrígan and Cú Chulainn after he reaches adulthood goes badly. When the Goddess offers herself to Cú Chulainn, he replies that he is too busy and turns down her offer of help in battle, saying, *"I didn't come here for a woman's backside."*[17]

This angers the Morrígan, who then tells Cú Chulainn that she will attack him in three different forms whilst he is fighting his enemies. She will attack him as an eel, a she-wolf and as a cow. He responds by telling her that he will wound her each time, and that she will not be healed of the wounds until he blesses her, which he will refuse to do.

The idea that a hero should threaten a Goddess might seem strange, and even stranger that he should be capable of wounding her, until we take into account Cú Chulainn's parentage – he is the son of Lugh, the God of Light, and is thus effectively a demi-God himself.

---

[16] *Tochmarc Emire* (The Wooing of Emer).
[17] *Táin Bó Cúailnge.*

The Morrígan's Cow Theft

The alternative first meeting between the Morrígan and the adult Cú Chulainn given in a different version of the story also goes inauspiciously.[18] Cú Chulainn lay asleep in Dun Imrid when he was woken by a cry from the North, a cry that was terrible and fearful to his ears (the shrieks of the Morrígan). He wakes so suddenly that he falls out of his bed unto the ground like a sack.

He rushes forth naked followed by his wife Emer, who brings with her his armour and clothes. Then he sees Laegh, his charioteer, in a harnessed chariot coming towards him from the North, who has also been disturbed by the noise. Cú Chulainn asks from which direction he heard the sound, and Laegh tells him it came from the North West.[19]

The two ride towards the sound and reach Ath de Fertá (*"The Ford of the Two Chariot Poles"*). When they arrive there, they see before them a chariot harnessed with a chestnut horse. The horse has one leg, and one eye, and one ear, and the pole of the chariot passes right through its body, so that the peg in front meets the halter, which passes through its forehead - a description which clearly indicates the otherworldly nature of the encounter.

Within the chariot sat a fearsome woman, with red eyebrows, and a crimson mantle wrapped about her. This mantle fell behind her between the wheels of the chariot, so that it swept along the ground. Walking beside the chariot was a big powerfully built man. He also wore a coat of crimson colour, and upon his back he carried a forked staff of white hazel wood. This man drove before him a fine glossy coated cow.

That this is the Morrígan is indicated to the reader by a number of symbols. In addition to the otherworldly horse, the red colouring of her hair and the regal red mantle following as a train all imply her sovereignty and association with war.

The red and white colours of the man again shows the otherworldly nature of this encounter, as is the reference to the forked staff of white hazelwood, the most magical of woods in Celtic myths and associated

---

[18] *Táin Bó Regamna.*

[19] Note the traditional direction for shades and spirits – a natural place for the Phantom Queen.

with wisdom. It is also noteworthy that hazel is the ninth letter in the Ogham alphabet, indicating further magical associations of the number nine and the Goddess.

Cú Chulainn challenges the man about the cow, as it is his task to guard the cows of Ulster. The Morrígan replies scathingly to him, saying, "So ... you would be a druid and give decisions about the law of cattle ownership? You are taking too much upon yourself, Cú Chulainn."[20]

Cú Chulainn becomes frustrated and demands to know why the woman addresses him when he is speaking to the man, and then demands the man's name. The man refuses to speak. Instead he is given a response in the form of a sequence of nonsensical words from the Morrígan as the man's name.

He then turns to her, demanding her name at which the man speaks and says her name is *"Fóebor becbéoil coimm diúir, folt scenb, gairit sceo úath"* which means: *"sharp-edged little mouth, emaciated body, spiked hair, a short and ghastly time."*[21]

The Morrígan exercises her right (under old Irish law) as a woman to answer the questions put, thus mocking Cú Chulainn and making him angry. Overcome with anger, Cú Chulainn feels he is being made a fool of and makes a great leap, straight into the woman's chariot. He lands with his feet upon her shoulders, and puts his sharp edged spear against the parting of her flame red hair.

She chastises him for threatening her and he again demands her true name. The Morrígan then tells him that she is a female poet and satirist, taking the cow as her reward for a fine poem from Dáire mac Fiachna of Cúailnge.

Cú Chulainn then demands to hear the poem, which she agrees to recite, but tells him to first get off her and out of her chariot. She then recites the poem, after which Cú Chulainn prepares to leap into the chariot again with his spear, but horse, man, chariot, and cow, have all disappeared, leaving only a crow.

Realising at last who she was, Cú Chulainn declares that if he had known her identity they would not have parted in such an unbefitting

---

[20] *Táin Bó Regamna.*
[21] *Táin Bó Regamna.*

manner, suggesting that he realised the brashness of his actions. Cú Chulainn and the Morrígan banter verbally and the Morrígan as the crow tells him: *"I am guarding your death and will continue to guard it."*[22] This statement is nicely ambiguous and can be taken in a positive or a negative manner, or indeed both.

The Battle of Cú Chulainn and Lóch

Later in the saga of Cú Chulainn his role as protector of Ulster's cattle again takes precedence. Queen Medb of Connacht covets the legendary Donn of Cúailnge (the Brown Bull of Ulster), which she wishes to mate with her herd. She tries to obtain the bull by offering sexual favours and gifts, but when this fails she decides to resort to cattle-raiding.

The men of Ulster are afflicted by a curse (the *ces noinden*, made long before by Macha) that causes them to be incapacitated when they are most needed for battle, leaving Cú Chulainn alone to hold off Queen Medb's army. After Cú Chulainn has single-handedly held off the forces of Queen Medb for several days, the Queen manipulates the hero Lóch into fighting Cú Chulainn.

Whilst Cú Chulainn and Lóch are fighting at a ford, the Morrígan attacks him three times, as she previously warned him she would. The first time she takes the form of a hornless white cow with red ears and he shatters one of her eyes. White and red animals symbolised the underworld in Celtic myth, so her otherworldly nature is being indicated here.

Next she attacks Cú Chulainn as a great black eel, large enough to coil three times around his legs and immobilize him, allowing Lóch to wound him. In response he breaks the eel's ribs and smashes half of its head.

Finally the Morrígan attacks him as a grey-red wolf and bites Cú Chulainn in the arm. He shatters her remaining eye, and whilst he is distracted Lóch wounds him again. To finish the fight he uses the Gae Bolga spear and kills Lóch, but not before Lóch wounds him a third time.

---

[22] *Táin Bó Regamna.*

After the combat *"came the Morrígan, daughter of Ernmas, from the side in the guise of an old woman and in Cú Chulainn's presence she milked a cow with three teats."*[23]

By doing this the Morrígan tricks Cú Chulainn, who is *"maddened with thirst"*,[24] into healing her, as he blesses her after drinking from each teat, healing the wounds he inflicted. He soon realises that he has been tricked, but it is already too late.

The Morrígan in her guise of Cailleach has manipulated Cú Chulainn into healing her, using one of her magic cows. The magic elfin cow whose milk heals is a popular creature in Celtic folklore, also occurring in Welsh myth, see e.g. the Iola MSS (Manuscript).

Nemain's Assistance

The next day it is clear that the Morrígan has already forgiven Cú Chulainn. She appears in her guise of Nemain to help him by killing some of the opposing army. Cú Chulainn makes fearful shouts in defiance of the vast army from all over Ireland that is arrayed against him.

Nemain then makes shrieks in response to his: *"Nemain, the War Goddess, brought confusion on the host ... so that a hundred warriors of them fell dead that night of terror"*[25]

A frustrated Queen Medb then sends another hero, Fer Diad of the impenetrable skin, to fight Cú Chulainn. Fer Diad is an old childhood friend of Cú Chulainn and the two are very evenly matched. The two heroes fight for three days, and each night Cú Chulainn shares with Fer Diad the use of healing potions given to him by his father Lugh.

Then on the fourth day Cú Chulainn uses the Gae Bolga spear and kills his friend. Before using the spear Cú Chulainn is seriously wounded, and is rushed away by his wife and friends to the fortress of Emain Macha to recover.

---

[23] *Táin Bó Cúailnge.*
[24] *Táin Bó Cúailnge.*
[25] *Táin Bó Cúailnge.*

The Downfall of Cú Chulainn

The story *Aided Conn Culainn* continues the saga after the *Táin Bó Cúailnge* and tells of the downfall of Cú Chulainn. Queen Medb is determined to have her revenge on Cú Chulainn, who has decimated her best warriors. She enlists three sisters called the three Badbs, who are also said to be the daughters of the magician Cailitín. These sisters have been trained specifically to bring about the downfall of Cú Chulainn.

The three Badbs or daughters of Cailitín are described as being monstrous in appearance, and are sometimes accompanied by the three sons of Cailitín in later versions of the myth (they have already been killed by Cú Chulainn in earlier versions).

When the three Badbs arrive at Emain Macha they let out a huge cry (a phenomenon associated with the Morrígan) and then stage a phantom battle to try and entice Cú Chulainn out to fight. Some writers suggest that these Badbs are not linked to the Morrígan, but the use of the name *Badb* and a phantom battle suggests the "Phantom Queen".

When this fails one of the daughters tries to tempt him out. *"Then Badb daughter of Cailitín came. She came in the form of a crow above the chamber where Cú Chulainn was and spoke magic words and he said nothing."*[26]

The druid Conchobar then instructs the women of Ulster to take Cú Chulainn to Glenn na mbodhar (the *"Glen of the Deaf"*), so that he will not hear any disturbance, whilst the men of Ulster recover from the curse that prevents them fighting. The Badbs make so much noise that he still hears them, but he does not leave the glen because he has given his word to Niam, one of the noblewomen present.

To overcome this frustration, Badb appears as one of Niam's women and lures Niam and some of the other women out of the glen and casts a spell on them to prevent them from moving or interfering. Then she uses her magic to shape-shift, and appears to Cú Chulainn as Niam and recites a poem bemoaning her fate if he does not fight. This persuades him, and he leaves the glen, to return to Emain Macha, despite the attempts of druids and other women to try and persuade him to stay.

---

[26] *Aided Conn Culainn.*

On his journey he encounters the Morrígan as the Washer at the Ford. She is described as a *"pale-skinned, fair-haired maiden"*,[27] and a druid called Cathbad, who has accompanied him, describes and interprets her actions.

"Do you see Little Hound,[28] asked Cathbad, "Badb's daughter yonder, washing your spoils and armour? Mournfully, ever-sorrowfully she executes and tells of your fall, when she signifies your defeat before Medb's great host and the sorcery of the children of Cailitín."[29]

The Breaking of Cú Chulainn's Geis

Cú Chulainn however ignores this omen and continues on his journey. He meets three crones who are all blind in their left eyes standing before him on the road. This immediately tells us that it is the Goddess in triple form, and that she is performing malevolent magic by the blindness of the left eyes. She shames Cú Chulainn into eating dog flesh that she is cooking.

The flesh itself has been prepared on spits of rowan with poisons and spells. The use of rowan is significant as it is traditionally the tree that protects from sorcery and evil magic. That it is being used here indicates that the effect of negating the magical effects will not work in this instance – the Goddess is taking no chances here.

The crone also hands the meat to Cú Chulainn with her left hand, and he receives it with his left hand, showing an acceptance of the fact that this is an inescapable magical encounter. He subsequently loses the strength from the left side of his body as a result of eating the food.

Cú Chulainn is under a geis (binding stricture) never to eat dog flesh, and under another geis never to refuse food. So he will break a geis either way, and not realising it is dog he eats the flesh.

Another version of the same story tells the encounter slightly differently. In the alternative version he only meets one Badb. She

---

[27] *Aided Conn Culainn.*
[28] A nickname based on the translation of his name as "Hound of Culainn".
[29] *Aided Conn Culainn.*

attacks him with a skewer on which she had been cooking the young dog, and he loses half his power from the attack. This is because the dog's blood enters his, which counts as breaking his geis never to consume dog, his totem animal.

The Morrígan's Last Attempt to Save Cú Chulainn

In the earlier versions of the tale, when Cú Chulainn is due to go and fight in the battle that will kill him, the Morrígan tries to stop him, to save his life. She smashes his chariot so that he will not be able to go into battle. However Cú Chulainn recites a poem to his horse and persuades it to pull the broken chariot, taking him to his doom.

The Death of Cú Chulainn

Cú Chulainn goes to fight his final battle accompanied by his horse and charioteer. On the way there he is taunted by three of Queen Medb's bards, who threaten his honour, and as a result he is forced to kill them using all three of his spears.

Queen Medb's men gather the spears and give them to Lughaid the King of Munster and Leinster. Lughaid throws Cú Chulainn's three spears back at Cú Chulainn. The first spear kills his charioteer; the second spear kills his horse, and the third spear wounds Cú Chulainn in the stomach, causing his intestines to spill out.

Cú Chulainn then has his last laugh when a *"raven of the Badb"*[30] lands at his feet, and a loop of his intestines fall out of their wound and onto the raven who trips on them and falls over. This is black humour at its darkest indeed.

When he is dying Cú Chulainn ties himself to a standing stone to prevent himself from dying sitting or lying down, as this would not be a hero's death. As he is dying a crow comes and sits on his shoulder. When Lughaid cuts off his head, despoiling the body, Cú Chulainn's sword slips and cuts off the king's arm. This is the Morrígan fulfilling her promise to guard his death.

---

[30] *Táin Bó Cúailnge.*

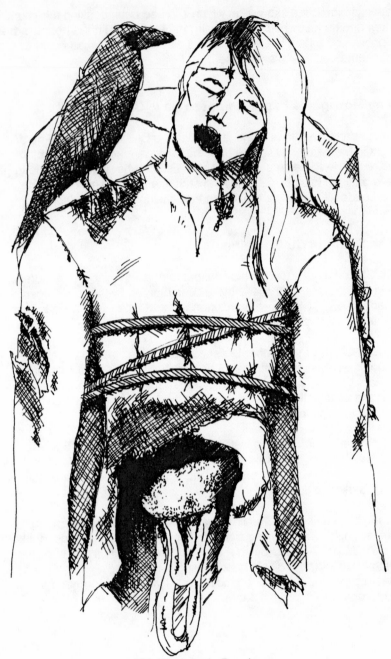

Cú Chulainn's Demise

The Avenging of Cú Chulainn

After the Ulstermen have recovered, they are led by the hero Conall
Cernach and decimate the army that killed Cú Chulainn. Conall
places Cú Chulainn's head, along with the *"stakes of the Badb"*[31] all
around a meadow. These are the severed heads of all the men he
has killed to avenge Cú Chulainn.

---

[31] A similar practice to the *"Macha's mast"* mentioned later.

2. Morrígan, Nemain, Badb and Macha

The best known guises of the Morrígan are Nemain, Badb and Macha. In various manuscripts and stories they are associated with each other, sometimes as sisters, and sometimes as guises of the same goddess. The term Morrígna was often used to describe these plural forms of the Morrígan.

"one of the three Morrígna, that is Macha and Badb and Morrígan."[32]

Sometimes the connection between the different guises is made very obvious: *"In the Wood of the Badb, i.e. of the Morrígan."*[33] At other times we see a chain of connections, with different guises being equated to the same role, such as being the wife of the Battle God Néit.

"She is the Badb of battle and is called Bé Néit "'the wife of Néit'."[34]

"Néit, i.e. the God of Battle. Nemain is his wife."[35]

In Celtic tales it was common for a Goddess to be expressed in different guises, to demonstrate more of her qualities. This most often took the form of familial relationship – i.e. as mother and daughter, or sisters. By examining the essence of the myths, and also viewing the picture as a whole, it becomes clear quite how many guises are assumed by the Morrígan.

Although these names represent the same essential Goddess, we nevertheless need to examine them separately to explore the different qualities being expressed through them. In doing so it quickly becomes obvious quite how universal the Morrígan was in her range of attributes. Indeed we may liken her to a Celtic Isis (the Egyptian Goddess often referred to as the Goddess of Ten Thousand Names), being the prime Goddess, of whom many others can easily be seen as guises to express her complexity and scope.

One important question that must be considered about the Morrígan when looking at the myths is which family of gods does she belong to?

---

[32] *Trinity H.3.18*
[33] *Tochmarc Emire*, 10th century.
[34] *Tochmarc Emire*.
[35] *Cormac's Glossary*.

A deduction can be made from the evidence that she is the bridge between the Túatha Dé Danann and the Fomorians, partaking of both families of deities.

The link to the Fomorians is indicated in several ways. Firstly, the word *mor* is only found in two places, these being the name of the Morrígan, and the name Fomorian. In some manuscripts[36] Néit (one of the Morrígan's husbands) is said to be the grandson of Balor, King of the Fomorians, hinting at a closer link. Also the Goddess Fea, a guise of the Morrígan, is referred to as Balor's daughter.[37]

Boann is also a daughter of Balor, and can be seen as a guise of the Morrígan, as will be explored subsequently. When asked of her powers before the Second battle of Moytura, the Morrígan says: *"I shall destroy those I have my eye on."*[38] In light of the connection between Fea, Boann and the Morrígan, this intriguing comment could be another way to imply her kinship to Balor, whose eye destroys any living thing it gazes upon.

However as will be clearly shown later, Danu is also connected with the Morrígan, and indeed was seen as part of the same complex Goddess. In some sources the Morrígan is even referred to as Danu, from whom the Túatha Dé Danann (children of Danu) are named,[39] showing that the Morrígan may be seen in the role of the mother of the Túatha Dé Danann gods.

---

[36] Versions of *Cath Maige Tuired* and *Cath Muighe Tuireadh*.
[37] *Banshenchas.*
[38] *Cath Maige Tuired.*
[39] *The Book of Lecan.*

Morrígan

"Who is stronger than hope? Death.
Who is stronger than the will? Death.
Stronger than love? Death.
Stronger than life? Death.
But who is stronger than death? Me, evidently.
Pass, Crow."[40]

The name Morrígan first occurs in Irish literature in 876/7. Her name is found in a glossary to the Books of the Old Testament, referring to Isaiah 34:14. The word *lamia* is described as *"monstrum in femine figura .i. morigain"* (monster in female form, that is a Morrígan).[41]

Old Glossaries are a major source of reference about guises of the Morrígan. The use of terms to define (or gloss) was a common way of explaining meaning and giving context to words in translations of religious and classical texts.

The connection with the Lamia is interesting, as this recalls a carving of three Lamiae at the Roman fort of Benwell in Northern Britain. The Lamiae were beautiful phantom women who seduced men, and killed them for their flesh and blood. That the Lamiae are in triple form and at a military fort suggests a connection to the Morrígan.

Other such descriptions in subsequent glossaries include reference to the Morrígan in association with horrible things: *"Gúdeman. i.e. horrors and Morrígna"*[42], and *"Gudomain, i.e. hooded crows, or women from the síd; lying wolves, that is, the false demons, the morrígna ... they are not demons of hell but demons of the air."*[43]

We can see here a common Christian approach to a deity who could not be neatly fitted into sainthood and assimilated into Christianity.

A number of translations have been suggested for the name Morrígan itself. The word *rígan* unquestionably means "queen", and is the root

---

[40] From *Examination at the Womb-door* in *Crow* by Ted Hughes (1930-1998).
[41] *MSS Regina 215.*
[42] *Cormac's Glossary*, 9th-12th century."
[43] *Trinity H.3.18.*

of the name Rigatona, meaning great queen. The name Rigatona is itself the root of the name Rhiannon, a connection that we will explore later.

The first part of the name, *mor*, has been given a number of alternate possible translations. All of these translations have some relevance to the different aspects of the Morrígan, so let us consider each of them.

Mor-rígan can be read as *"Great Queen"*, *"Terrible Queen"*, *"Phantom Queen"*, *"Faery Queen"*, *"Queen of Death"*, *"Sea Queen"* or *"Witch Queen"*. Great or Terrible Queen are the most commonly used meanings of her name, but as Queen of the Faery, Goddess of the Waters and Goddess of the Land all the other possibilities can be used as sources of inspiration and connection to her.

From the 11th century we see the Morrígan being equated with classical figures whose names are incorporated into the Irish tales. So we see her equated with the Greek Fury Alecto: *"Allecto came for a while, that is, the Morrígan, in the form of a bird which perched on the pillar-stone."*[44]

---

[44] *Táin Bó Cúailnge Rescension I.*

Badb

"As I was walking all alaine,
I heard twa corbies making a mane;
The tane unto the t'other say,
'Where sall we gang and dine to-day?'
'In behint yon auld fail dyke,
I wot there lies a new-slain knight;'"[45]

Badbh, Badbdh or Badb means *"Crow"* or *"Raven"* and refers to a group of Goddesses, not a single individual. She feeds on the carrion on the battlefield, and can be seen as the devouring aspect, clearing away the outdated form to make way for new growth.

"The red-mouth Badb will cry around the house.
For bodies it will be solicitous. Pale Badbs shall shriek.
Badbs will be over the breasts of men ...."[46]

She was often referred to as Badbh Catha, meaning *"the Battle Crow"*, describing the hooded crows that were often seen feasting at the battlefield. Badb usually appeared in crow or hag form.

"In the Wood of the Badb, i.e. of the Morrígan. For that is her wood,
i.e. the land of Ross, and she is the Badb of battle and is called Bé
Néit "'the wife of Néit'."[47]

In this tale from the Ulster cycle Badb is unequivocally described as being the Morrígan, and also the wife of Néit, the God of Battle, of whom little beyond a name is known.

From around the 10th century the name Badb becomes interchangeable in some texts with *fúir* (Fury) and *bandea* (Goddess) in connection with the Greek Fury Tesiphone. She becomes seen as representing the classical Greek image of the Fury and is also

---

[45] From *Twa Corbies* (Two Crows) – traditional Scottish 14th century ballad. Corbie is the old Scottish name for a crow or raven.
[46] *Bruiden da Chocae*, (The destruction of Da Choca's Hostel) 15th century.
[47] *Tochmarc Emire*, 10th century.

equated with other War Goddesses such as the Roman Bellona in translations of classical texts.[48]

Badb turns up a number of times in *Cath Catharda* (The Civil War), which is book one of the seven volumes of the Roman writer Lucan's *Pharsalia*. Here there seems to be a subtle process of equation to the Medusa going on as well, with reference to *"her serpentine, venomous locks."*

"The Badb of battle was seen each night, her pine firebrand flaming red in her hand and her serpentine, venomous locks rustling around her head, urging the Romans to battle."[49]

Later in the text Caesar is equated with both Bellona (Roman War Goddess) and Badb, who are also equated to each other.[50] The latter is interesting in light of the reference in the early thirteenth century French tale of *Huon of Bordeaux*, where Oberon is described as the child of Morgan Le Fay and Julius Caesar.

"Caesar began to display his royal deeds in the battle. Heat and vigour, eagerness and fury and rage and frenzy of mind and spirit permeated him … so that there was no one like him but the Badb of battle, who is around the battle with scourges in her hand, inducing the hosts to conflict … Wherever he moves, like Bellona brandishing her bloody scourge."

The medusa inference made by translators in texts is even more explicit in *The Thebaid of Statius*:

"As they saw the diabolical, forbidding countenance of that raging, red-mouthed Badb … Then a hundred venomous, spiteful horned serpents with stingers rose up around her head … Then she arose and brandished the venomous snake which was in her hand at the hosts."[51]

A medieval Irish text, translated from Latin, even puts Badb in the Trojan War, as the bearer of news, reminiscent of the Badb spreading the victory tidings after the battle with the Fomorians: *"Crows [badba]*

---

[48] *Togail na Tebe: The Thebaid of Statius*
[49] *Dearbairdi in Catha Catharda* (The Sure Signs of the Civil War).
[50] Note both Badb and Bellona being described as bearing scourges.
[51] We may observe here the serpents are described as horned, which is a particularly popular Celtic motif.

rose over their heads in order to scatter tidings of them and tell their deeds throughout Asia and Europe.[52]

By the late 14th century the word *badb* is being used synonymously with the word *Cailleach*, a guise which is discussed in its own chapter.[53] The word has also been used as a derogatory term to insult people, in the form *a bhaidhbh*, with the meaning of *"thou witch"*.[54]

---

[52] *Togail Troí.*
[53] For an example of this see *Caithréimm Thoirdhealbhaigh*, 14th century.
[54] *Dictionary of the Irish Language*, 1913.

Macha

Macha means *"Pasture"*, *"Field"* or *"Plain"*, and is a clear reference to a manifestation of the Goddess as the land in her earthy guise, and possibly also alluding to a guise as a Horse Goddess (giving links to Rhiannon and Epona). She is a champion of the power of all women, demonstrating her superiority to boastful men when challenged.

As a guise of the Morrígan, she is more savage, being described in an old manuscript[55] thus:

"Macha, that is a crow; or it is one of the three Morrígna, that is Macha and Badb and Morrígan. Whence Mesrad Machae, Macha's mast, that is the heads of men after their slaughter. As Dub Ruise said: There are rough places yonder, where men cut off Macha's mast; where they drive young calves into the fold; where the raven-women instigate battle.[56]

Apart from the collection of severed heads, where the soul was believed to reside, which can be seen as akin to the Norse Valkyries; we can also see the reference to driving off cattle clearly refers to the cattle-raiding enjoyed so much by this Goddess.

So not only does Macha "instigate battle", suggesting her role as the inciter and use of words or sound to encourage battle, but she also claims her dues after the fighting is over – the souls (severed heads) of the best warriors amongst the slain. And of course the hooded crows and ravens would be seen on the battlefield eating carrion after any battle.

Macha was a triple Goddess in that she is described as having three different depictions in semi-divine or mortal form. The first of these is as the wife of Nemedh ("Sacred One"), whence she was a prophetess who foretold the destruction of the country to be wrought in the future Táin conflict. Her husband named a plain after her, and she died of a broken heart when she saw what devastation would be wrought there by the Táin.

---

[55] *Trinity H.3.18.*

[56] The version in *Cormac's Glossary* is shorter and variously dated between the 9th-12th century: *Macha, that is a crow; or it is one of the three Morrígna, Mesrad Machae, Macha's mast, that is the heads of men after their slaughter.*

The second depiction is as the divine (though mortal) bride of Crunnchu, when she cursed the Ulstermen. Here she punishes the folly of men, laying the foundations for future events (the circumstances which cause the death of Cú Chulainn as he had to fight alone without the Ulstermen).

Crunnchu (or Cruinn) is a wealthy farmer, and one day the beautiful Macha turns up and marries him. She brings great prosperity and his crops all do extremely well (hinting at the bountiful Earth Goddess), but she warns him that he must never boast about her.

Crunnchu of course does not listen to Macha, and boasts that his wife could run so swiftly that she could even outrun the king's horses (again very suggestive of a Horse Goddess connection). The king hears about this boast and imprisons Crunnchu. The king tells Macha that the only way to save her husband is to run in the horse race at the great Ulster Assembly.

Macha appeals to the king and the crowd to let her deliver her babies before she runs, appealing to them saying *"A mother bore each one of you"*. Even though nine months pregnant, Macha was forced to run, and she warned that she would curse Ulster for what they were doing to her. She won, but died giving birth to twins.[57]

With her dying breath she cursed the Ulstermen with the *ces noinden*, the weakness curse that caused them to become as helpless as a woman in childbirth for five days and four nights whenever their strength was needed most. This curse would last for nine generations.[58]

It is also worth noting that Cú Chulainn's horse was called the "Grey of Macha", and when he went to harness it to his chariot on the day of his death, it wept tears of blood.

The third depiction was as the divine legendary warrior-ruler of Ireland, Macha Mongruad – "Macha of the Red Tresses". The tale of the founding of the site of Emain Macha ("the Twins of Macha")

---

[57] This tale is recounted in *"Noínden Ulad 7 Emuin Macha"* (The Debility of the Ulstermen and the Twins of Macha). This text may date back to the mid 9th century, and certainly no later than the 10th century.

[58] See chapter 9 *The Witch Goddess* for the text of the curse.

demonstrates the goddess emphasising the presumption of men seeking to deny the sovereign right of women as guardians of the land. She was challenged by the five sons of Dithorba, and visits them feasting after a hunt, disguised in the form of a leper.

Even though she was in the form of a leper and repellant, all of the men desired her. Macha Mongruad slept with each man in turn, overcoming them and enslaving them, and forcing them to build the stronghold which was named after her.[59]

In *Cormac's Glossary* a description is given which implies her divine nature. He writes, *"Thus was the outline of the fort described by the woman (Queen Macha), when she was sitting she took her pin from her garment to measure around her with her pin."*

This description implies gigantic stature to Macha Mongruad, indicating divine nature, in the same way that the gigantic form of the Morrígan and Daghda when they have sex indicates their divine and superior nature.

Macha is described as being married to the ex-king of the Túatha Dé Danann, Nuada, who lost his hand in the First Battle of Moytura.[60] In the Second Battle of Moytura, Macha and Nuada are killed by Balor when he opens his all-destroying eye. However she re-appears in subsequent tales, so her death does not seem to be a permanent event.

---

[59] MSS *RIA 23 N10.*
[60] *Cath Maige Tuired.*

Nemain

"But Fury was ill apparelèd
In rags, that naked nigh she did appear,
With ghastly looks and dreadful drerihed;[61]
And from her back her garments she did tear,
And from her head oft rent her snarled hair:"[62]

Nemain means *"Frenzy"*, *"Panic"* or *"Venomous"*, and indicates the battle fury of the Warrior Goddess, intimidating the side that was going to lose with her shrieks, and exhorting the side she had decided would win to victory.

Nemain is described in *Cormac's Glossary*, as the wife of Néit, further emphasizing the interchangeability and connection of these different guises of the Morrígan: *"Néit, i.e. the God of battle. Nemain is his wife"*; *"Bé Néit ... Nemon was his wife. This couple was venomous indeed."*[63]

Nemain is directly identified with Badb in later texts: *"Nemain, i.e. the Badb of battle, or a hooded crow."*[64] She is also mentioned in a stanza with Fea, further indicating the connection to this little-known guise: *"Banba, Fotla, and Fea, Nemain of prophetic stanzas, Danu, mother of the Gods."*[65]

When Nemain shrieked at the Connacht army facing Cú Chulainn one hundred soldiers dropped dead with fright in the night. Before this she had promised both sides they would win, even though she had decided the Ulstermen would, she was also known for her (at times) fickle nature.

If we consider the deathly shriek combined with the prophecy of imminent death, we can see a clear parallel to the Banshee, indeed in Munster the Badb was referred to as the Bean Sìdhe (*"fairy woman"*) or Banshee.

---

[61] Another word for sorrowful.
[62] *The Faery Queen*, Book 3 Canto 12:17, Edmund Spenser (1553-1599).
[63] *Cormac's Glossary.*
[64] *Glossary*, Michael O'Clery, 1643.
[65] *Lebor Gabála Érenn (The Book of Invasions)*, 12th century.

Of course the side that she supported saw Nemain much more positively.

Accounts record the appearance of the Faery Queen Aoibheall as a banshee figure the night before the Battle of Clontarf in 1014, informing King Brían Bóru of his impending death.

The same accounts also describe the appearance of Nemain at the battle [66] where the High King Brían Bóru defeated the Vikings, she was seen to appear shrieking above the warriors' heads, instilling terror into the opposing Vikings and thus protecting her land from invasion.

It has been suggested that Nemain is linked to the British Goddess of the Sacred Grove, Nemetona. However apart from a similarity of name there is little to connect these two goddesses.

---

[66] *Cogadh Gaedhel re Gallaibh* (The War of the Gaedhil with the Gaill), 12th century, and *Annals of Lough Cé,* 13th century.

3. Wise Crone: Tales of the Cailleach

The Morrígan is also referred to as the Cailleach or Caillighe, which can mean *"veiled one"*, *"old woman/crone"* or *"nun"*. The early 9th century *Lament of the Old Woman of Beare*, written around 800, contains elements of Christian and Pagan myths merged together, which may be where this name with its dual Pagan and Christian meanings comes from.

In the lament she is the Cailleach Bearra, a crone, recounting a monologue of nostalgia for her youthful beauty and royal lovers. This image is clearly that of the Crone Goddess who represents the bestower of sovereignty to the king chosen to be the divine consort.

The Cailleach Beara was described as having two sisters, Cailleach Bolus and Cailleach Corca Duibune (giving the triple form often associated with the Morrígan), and she was wed to the God Lugh under the name of Bui (*Yellow*).

In the 14th century *Yellow Book of Lecan*, the Cailleach Beara is described as having seven youthful periods, marrying seven husbands, and having fifty foster-children who went on to found many tribes and nations. She was said to reside around the Beara peninsula, on the Cork-Kerry border.

With the similarity of her name to that of the Indian Goddess of Destruction Kali, it is interesting to observe here the symbolism of fifty, strongly associated with Kali as the fifty skulls around her neck which each depict a letter of the Sanskrit alphabet, and the fifty petals of the six major chakras from the base chakra to the third eye corresponding to the spinal column. We may also note another similarity in that Kali is often portrayed as blue-skinned, like the Cailleach.

A Scottish fragment of this tale has her as the Cailleach Bheur telling a prior's daughter in Tiree how far back her memory stretches when asked how old she is, *"And I saw Leinster lake in Ireland when children could swim across."* She also mentions *"the Raven's mound"*.[67]

In Scotland she was called Cailleach Bheur. The Cailleach Bheur had one eye in a visage of mackerel blue with red teeth. The blue-skinned

---

[67] *Popular Tales of the West Highlands* - J.F Campbell, 1860.

hag also occurs in literature, showing the survival of the image of figures like the Cailleach and Black Annis, e.g. John Milton in his seventeenth century *Comus, A Mask*: *"In fog or fire, by lake or Moorish fen, blue meager hag, or stubborn unlaid ghost."*

"Her heyre hang down about hyr hede,
The tane was black, the other hray,
Her eyne semyt onte before was grey,
Her gay clethyng was all away
Her body as blow [blue] as ony bede [bead]."[68]

She was the Queen of Winter and, at winter's end, she drank from the Well of Youth. The waters transformed her into the Queen of Summer, a beautiful maiden. This seasonal change suggests an Earth Goddess whose form changes with the seasons.

Sir Walter Scott describes the change back from maiden to crone at the end of the summer graphically:
"The appearance of the beautiful lady is changed into that of the most hideous hag in existence; one side is blighted and wasted, as if by palsy; one eye drops from her head; her colour, as clear as virgin silver, is now of a dun, leaden hue."[69]

Another version of the myth has Cailleach Bheur keeping the princess Bride captive in her cave in Ben Nevis, forcing her to wash Bheur's mantle. Bride eventually escapes with the help of Angus, King of Summer, who she marries. Here, the Cailleach Bheur represents winter and Bride summer.

Cailleach Bheur, by keeping Bride captive actually keeps the spring from rising in a similar way to the myth of the Greek Goddess Persephone, except that Persephone's lover Hades represents winter rather than summer.

In yet another different version of the myth she is reborn on every All Hallows Eve (Samhain) as the Winter Goddess returning to bring the winter and the snows. She carries a magical staff, which freezes the ground with every tap.

---

[68] *Minstrelsy of the Scottish Border* – Sir Walter Scott, 1802.
[69] *Letters on Demonology and Witchcraft* – Sir Walter Scott, 1831, letter 4:129.

She also guards the animals throughout the winter, and returns to the earth by turning to stone on Beltane Eve. The stone she turned into was said to remain *"always moist"*.[70]

Before turning to stone she would throw her magic staff under a holly tree or gorse bush, which were her sacred plants. A local verse explains that this is why grass does not grow under holly trees: *"She threw it beneath the hard holly tree, where grass or hair has never grown."*[71]

One tale has the Cailleach ushering in winter by washing her huge plaid in the Corryvreckan whirlpool, one of her sacred sites.

"Before the washing the roar of a coming tempest is heard by people on the coast for a distance of twenty miles, and for a period of three days before the cauldron boils. When the washing is over the plaid of old Scotland is virgin white."[72]

Of all the animals the deer are most beloved of the Cailleach. She treats them as her cattle, herding and milking them and protecting them from hunters. However she also protects wild pigs and boars, wild goats, wild cattle and wolves.

A local tale from Sutherland in Scotland tells how a deer is killed after it eats an enchanted blue cord that is a counter-spell to the protective magic of the Cailleach. We may see in this the idea of the necessary cull of the herd being allowed by the Cailleach.

"They [the deer] were standing all about the door of the hut till one of them ate a hank of blue worsted hung from a nail in it. The Cailleach struck the animal and said: 'The spell is off you; and Lord Reay's bullet will be your death today.' William repeated this to his master to confirm the tale of his having passed the night in the hut of the great hag, which no one would believe. And the event justified it, for a fine yellow hind was killed that day, and the hank of blue yarn was found in his stomach."[73]

---

[70] *Scottish Folk Lore and Folk Life* – Donald MacKenzie, 1935, p138.
[71] *Witchcraft and Second Sight in the Scottish Highlands* – J.G. Campbell, 1902, p254.
[72] *Myth, Tradition and Story from Western Argyll* – K.W. Grant, 1925, p8,
[73] *Popular Tales of the West Highlands* - J.F Campbell, 1860, vol 2, tale 27.

A local Scottish legend has the Cailleach transforming into a heron.[74] There are variants of this where she turns into a cormorant, eagle or gull. All are in keeping with the avian connection and shape-shifting abilities of the Morrígan.

The Cailleach is described as "Gentle Annie" (see also Black Annis) by the sailors of Cromarty, to placate her. The sudden storms which blow up there are considered to be her playing tricks with the weather. She is referred to in eighteenth century records from Strathlachlan as "The Old Wife of Thunder" due to her ability to command the weather at her pleasure.

The most extreme form of this weather aspect is when she comes down from Lochlann in a dark cloud and throws down thunderbolts and lightning, which set the forests of Scotland on fire.[75]

The Cailleach Bheur is referred to as *"the daughter of Grianan"* or *"Grianaig"* (little Sun). Little Sun was a term used to refer to winter, as opposed to the Big Sun which referred to summer. This describes the old concept of there being only two seasons – summer and winter.

Summer was seen as lasting from Beltane to Samhain and winter from Samhain to Beltane. Beltane, or May Day, is 1st May, and Samhain is 1st November. These are also the times when the veil between the worlds of life and death is said to be thinnest, and when the faery court move between their summer and winter palaces.

Some versions have the Cailleach ruling between the Equinoxes, from Autumn Equinox to Spring Equinox. The Equinoxes are the days of the year when there is an equal amount of light and darkness in the day, so this period is the half of the year when there is more darkness in the day than light. The Spring Equinox is usually on 21st or 22nd March, and the Autumn Equinox on 21st or 22nd September. 25th March was referred to as *Latha na Caillich* (Cailleach Day), and is now sometimes known as "Lady Day".

There are several stories told about her in connection to particular places. One story connected her to a well on the summit of Ben Cruachan in Argyll. Every sunset she capped the flowing water with a

---

[74] *Short Sketches of the Wild Sports and Natural History of the Highlands* – C. St. John, 1846, chapter 3.
[75] *Transactions of the Gaelic Society of Inverness* Volume 26:277-9.

large flat stone and then released it at sunrise. Again the transformation of state between light and dark is indicated, with the flow of water during day (equating to summer) and the staunching of the flow during the night (equating to winter).

One night, when she was weary from driving her goats across the mountains, she fell asleep at the side of the well. Without her to stop the flow, the water gushed forth, breaking through at the Pass of Brander. This created Loch Awe, and drowned local people and cattle in its wake.[76]

She was so horrified by her mistake that she turned to stone. The overflowing well is a common folklore motif, used to explain the formation of many lakes and lochs. The turning to stone in other versions of the myth is found in this story again, and both this and the control of water point to the Cailleach as being an Earth Goddess.

Many of the aspects of the Cailleach can be found in the nineteenth century poem Cailleach Bein-Y-Vreich:

---

[76] *Myth, Tradition and Story from Western Argyll* – K.W. Grant, 1925.

"Weird wife of Bein-y-Vreich! horo! horo!
Aloft in the mist she dwells;
Vreich horo! Vreich horo! Vreich horo!
All alone by the lofty wells.
Weird, weird wife! with the long grey locks,
She follows her fleet-foot stags,
Noisily moving through splinter'd rocks,
And crashing the grisly crags.
Tall wife, with the long gray hose! in haste
The rough stony beach she walks;
But dulse or seaweed she will not taste,
Nor yet the green kail stalks.
And I will not let my herds of deer,
My bonny red deer go down;
I will not let them down to the shore,
To feed on the sea-shells brown.
Oh, better they love in the corrie's recess,
Or on mountain top to dwell,
And feed by my side on the green, green cress,
That grows by the lofty well.
Broad Bein-y-Vreich is grisly and drear,
But wherever my feet have been
The well-springs start for my darling deer,
And the grass grown tender and green.
And there high up on the calm nights clear,
Beside the lofty spring,
They come to my call, and I milk them there,
And a weird wild song I sing.
But when hunter men round my dun deer prowl,
I will not let them nigh;
Through the rended cloud I cast one scowl,
They faint on the heath and die.
And when the north wind o'er the desert bare
Drives loud, to the corries below
I drive my herds down, and bield them there
From the drifts of the blinding snow.
Then I mount the blast, and we ride full fast,
And laugh as we stride the storm,
I, and the witch of the Cruachan Ben,
And the scowling-eyed Seul-Gorm."[77]

---

[77] Cailleach Bein-Y-Vreich - John Campbell Shairp (1819–85),
published 1895.

In the tale of Diarmaid hunting the wild boar, the Cailleach is referred to as *Mala Liath* (Grey Eyebrows) and is the protectress of swine. The herd motif is a common one for different guises of the Morrígan, whether it is a herd of cows, deer or swine that she looks after.

Nobody had managed to kill the venomous boar, but Diarmaid tracks it to its lair. On the way a raven pecking a hare's corpse and a crow on a boulder both warn him off.

The raven tells him that he will kill the boar but die in the process, and the crow tells him to return to his wife Grainne, who he had eloped with, otherwise he would die in combat with the boar.

Mala Lia follows him and taunts him and curses him, urging him to return to Grainne. Diarmaid throws her over a cliff and fights the boar. He kills it but is slain by a venomous bristle, which pierces the inside of one of his heels.

This tale suggests earlier roots, with the choice between the old crone of winter Mala Lia and the maiden of summer Grainne. Mala Lia tries to persuade Diarmaid to return to his summer maiden, appearing as both a crow and a raven, foretelling his death. But he is headstrong and will not listen to her, and pays the price by dying after fighting the poisonous boar (representing the quest to kill the monstrous creature that is found in many tales).

Another form of the Cailleach that is reminiscent of Black Annis is the Gyre Carling (Gay Old Wife), described in private correspondence by Sir Walter Scott as the *"mother witch of the Scottish peasantry"*. In the correspondence Scott quoted the following lines from a poem in the Bannatyne MSS describing her unpleasant tastes:

"Thair dwelt ane grit Gyre Carling in awld Betokis bour,
That levit [lived] upoun menis flesche [men's flesh]."

Gyre Carling carried an iron club (*"ane yren club"*), which we can equate with the rod of winter carried by the Cailleach Bheur. When she is attacked by dogs she shape-shifted into a pig, demonstrating another of the abilities associated with this Goddess.

"The Carling schup [shaped] her on ane sow and is her gaitis [road] gane,

Grunting our [over] the Greik sie [Greek Sea]."[78]

The Manx version of the Cailleach is called the Caillagh ny Gromagh (Old Woman of Gloominess). Like one of the Scottish versions, this Cailleach is a weather spirit with overtones of her older role as Earth Goddess.

If St Bride's Day is fine, she comes out to gather sticks to keep her warm for the rest of the summer. If it is wet she stays in, and has to improve the weather if she wants to come out. A fine 1st February is therefore a bad omen. She is sometimes seen in the shape of a giant bird when she gathers sticks, recalling the avian connection to Badb.

The ninth century Christian hagiography, *The Life of St Samson of Dol* has a significant reference to the Cailleach in it. First however we may note that Samson is born to a previously barren woman, after her husband is told to present her with a silver rod equal to her height.

The husband, Amon, gives his wife three silver rods each equal to her height. We can see here the use of the faery metal silver, and also the triple motif. The wife and mother is called Anna, which may well be derived from Anu. Anna is visited by God in a vision, who tells her she will have a special child who *"Shall be holy and a high priest before Almighty God."*[79]

When St Samson is travelling one day he hears a dreadful shriek (reminiscent of the cries of the Morrígan), and sees a sorceress: *"in truth a very old woman with shaggy hair and that already grey, with her garments of red, holding in her hand a bloody trident."*[80] This woman, who is clearly representing the Cailleach (her age, hair and red garments are all appropriate motifs) is chasing a man to death.

Of course as the hero St Samson commands her to stop in the name of Jesus and questions her. It is significant that as well as identifying herself as a sorceress, the woman also says *"I have eight sisters"*,[81] recalling the sacred number nine associated with the Goddess throughout the Celtic myths. The sorceress will not change her ways and so is killed by St Samson.

---

[78] *MSS Bannatyne.*
[79] *Life of St. Samson of Dol* – Thomas Taylor, 1925.
[80] *Life of St. Samson of Dol.*
[81] *Life of St. Samson of Dol.*

4. The Queen of Battle

The main form of warfare in Dark Age and Medieval Ireland was cattle-raiding. In literature this is referred to as a *táin* ("driving-off"). The Morrígan as Queen of Battle loved to be present at such raids and the resulting battles to enjoy the slaughter and gather her harvest of warriors.

The druid Dubhdiadh described her presence at the Battle of Magh-Rath:

"Over his head is shrieking
A lean hag quickly hopping
Over the points of their weapons and shields
She is the grey-haired Morrígan."[82]

Indeed if there was no battle going on, she would not hesitate to start one, as is demonstrated by the *Cattle Raid of Cooley*, which she initiates by stealing a magical cow. Some might find it strange that the Celts should worship a Goddess of Battle, but Celtic women could be every bit as ferocious as their men. By law a daughter who inherited land from her mother in the absence of a male heir was liable to military service, a practice that was abolished by Saint Adamnán in the eight century.

Roman writers frequently recorded details of Celtic women taking part in battles, and seemed to think very highly of them. *"If he calls in his wife, stronger than he by far and with flashing eyes; least of all when she swells her neck and gnashes her teeth, and poising her white arms, proceeds to rain punches mingled with kicks, like shots discharged by the twisted cords of a catapult."*[83]

As well as mythical figures like Queen Medb, who was a war leader and warrior queen, we have the famous example of Queen Boudicca of the Iceni. Tacitus recorded that there were women fighting in the British forces that massacred the inhabitants of three Roman cities before being defeated.[84]

---

[82] *Cath Muighe Rath*, 12th century.
[83] Ammianus Marcellinus 14.12.1.
[84] Tacitus, *Annals* 14.36.

At the Roman assault on Anglesey in 61 CE, women were prominent in the defence of the sacred groves of the Druids: *"On the shore stood the opposing [British] army with its dense array of armed warriors, while between the ranks dashed women in black attire like the Furies, with hair dishevelled, waving brands. All round the druids ... scared our soldiers."*[85]

It has been suggested that the mysterious British Goddess Andraste, invoked by Boudicca before attacking the Romans, and described as *"a savage warrior Goddess"* was actually the Morrígan. Dio Cassius in his *History of Rome* says that Andraste was the Icenians' name for *"Victory"*, recalling the Greek Goddess Nike, whose name also means Victory, and that Andraste enjoyed their especial reverence.

It is possible that as with many other names we now use this was a deity title rather than the true name, so this may have been a title of the Morrígan used by Boudicca to incite her troops, as we know that she was associated with the type of vocal encouragement before battle displayed by Boudicca when invoking Andraste.

Boudicca released a hare for Andraste before going into battle as a form of divination, if the hare ran in the right direction it indicated victory. This is why the hare is often given as sacred to Andraste.

The Morrígan would be present at battles in her guises of Badb and Nemain as well at these times, singing and killing men out of sheer fright. Such men were obviously not hero material.

A good example of this was during the night before a battle between the warriors of Connacht and the warriors of Ulster, when the Morrígan sowed strife and despondency between the camps, singing in darkness:

"The beak of the raven in the neck of men,
Blood will gush, flesh will be hacked.
Madness of battle, the warrior's storm,
Ruin descends on Cruachan's men,
Grief to Ireland, but to Ulster, all hail!" [86]

---

[85] Tacitus, *Annals* 14.30
[86] *Táin Bó Cúailnge.*

During the same night, Nemain and Badb summoned the men of the four provinces of Ireland to meet their fate on the fields of Garech and Ilgarech. When they heard this call, many died of fright.

Those who survived and fought on the field of battle then stood a chance of having their souls collected by her, in a similar manner to that of the Valkyries in Norse myth.

When the Celts went into battle, they would make a lot of noise first, shouting and shrieking, and banging their shields. This was also true when warriors were psyching themselves up for single combat.

"In addition, songs as they go into battle and yells and leapings and the dreadful din of arms as they clash shields according to some ancestral custom – all these are deliberately used to terrify their foes." [87]

During such times a warrior would sing praises of his own prowess and honour his family, and heap abuse on his opponent. This was known as "Boasting", and was seen as part of the build-up to a fight. *"When any man accepts the challenge to battle, they then break forth into a song of praise of the valiant deeds of their ancestors and in boast of their own high achievements."* [88]

In addition druids and bards were known to accompany war bands, inciting warriors to fight bravely with songs and odes, or shaming any who displayed cowardice.

After winning a single combat, the victor would often raise the severed head of the opponent and sing or whoop. [89] The severed heads collected by warriors after battles were known as *"Macha's Acorn Crop"*. This emphasises the Celtic belief in the location of the soul in the head. By collecting the heads of enemy warriors in the name of the Morrígan the victorious warriors believed they gained the bravery of their victims.

The Morrígan as Badb and Nemain is also associated with Néit, God of Battle. As Goddess of Battle this is no surprise, but it leads us to a further name that may indicate another of her guises. The Goddess

---

[87] Livy 38.17.4-5 (trans. Foster).
[88] Diodorus Siculus 5.28.3.
[89] Silius Italicus *4.213-25;* Diodorus Siculus *5.29.4.*

Fea is also described as the wife of Néit. The name Fea is variously translated as *"death"*, *"that which causes death"*, or *"to attack"*.[90]

---

[90] *O'Davoren's Glossary,* Trinity H.2.15, 16th century.

5. The Earth Goddess

The Morrígan is not usually considered as an Earth Goddess; nevertheless the evidence indicates that this is one of her major guises. A number of old texts refer to a link between the Morrígan and the Earth Goddess Danu (or Anu), even to the extent of equating them as the same Goddess.

As the Morrígan is often linked with rivers, it is worth noting in this context that the name Danu means "river", and may be the root of the name of the river Danube in Germany, where the Celts were known to live. The name Anu is also recorded in places as Anand and Anann, and likewise Danu as Danand and Danann (and hence Túatha Dé Danann).

There are several references to the different guises of the Morrígan as daughters of a mysterious female figure called Ernmas. This name literally means *"iron-death"*, and she is described as being a witch or sorceress. So in *The Book of Invasions* we find:

"Banba, Fotla and Fea, Neman of prophetic stanzas, Danu, mother of the Gods. Badb and Macha, greatness of wealth, Morrígan – source of enchantments, servants in her attendance, were the daughters of Ernmas."[91]

Within some of these texts the Morrígan is also connected with the Mother Goddess Anu or Danu. This is a conjunction that occurs a number of times, and is highly significant.

In *The Book of Leinster* we find Anu and the Morrígan being equated, in connection with a pair of hills (i.e. the land): *"Badb and Macha and Anu, i.e. the Morrígan, from whom the Paps of Anu in Luachair are named, were the three daughters of Ernmas the witch."*[92]

This theme is repeated in *The Book of Lecan*. Here Danu and the Morrígan are again equated, and this is extended to also refer to the whole pantheon: *"The Morrígan ... and it is from her other name "Danu" the Paps of Ana in Luchair are named, as well as the Túatha Dé Danann."*[93]

---

[91] *The Book of Invasions.*
[92] *The Book of Leinster.*
[93] *The Book of Lecan.*

If the Morrígan is also Danu, then this has major implications, for it then means that the Morrígan is the Mother of the Gods of this pantheon. We could then arguably call them the Túatha Dé Morrigu as well as or instead of the Túatha Dé Danann.

This view is confirmed by a significant foretelling in the lead-up to the *First Battle of Moytura*. The Fir Bolg king Eochaid has a prophetic dream that describes the invasion from the sea of the Túatha Dé Danann, which he asks his Druid to interpret for him.

"I saw a great flock of black birds coming from the depths of the ocean. They settled over all of us, and fought with the people of Ireland. They brought confusion on us and destroyed us. It seemed to me that one of us struck the noblest of the birds and cut off one of its wings."[94]

That the invading Túatha Dé Danann are described as a *"great flock of black birds"* clearly indicates that they are all connected to the Morrígan as her children. The cutting off of the wing of the noblest bird refers to Nuada's loss of his hand, removing his right to the kingship as he is no longer whole in body.

If we consider the Welsh Gods, we see that the Earth Goddess Don bears a distinct similarity to Danu, being the mother of the pantheon. The Welsh pantheon is known as the House of Don. Don is married to the Death God Beli, recalling Morrígan's marriage to Néit.

The name of the Goddess Macha meaning *"field"*, *"pasture"* or *"plain"* also hints at a connection with the land, for it refers to the very substance of the land itself.

The union of the Morrígan with the Daghda, who represented the earth, may be seen as a later version of this connection, with the Goddess giving her blessing to the God in his role as Earth and Fertility God.

Local Irish lore again illustrates how the reality of the Goddess' connection with the land is preserved, with the tradition of the Cally Berry, the Hag of the Harvest Festival made of oats.

---

[94] *Cath Muighe Tuireadh.*

A figure or plait of oats would be made with the last oats, and ritually severed with a sickle (c.f. the severed head), and placed around the neck of the woman of the house, as the guardian of the hearth (and as the representative of the Earth Goddess), then subsequently placed above the table looking down (giving her blessing) during the ensuing feast.

Shaping the Land

The local Irish legends of the Cailleach Beara (from whom the Cally Berry is derived) show the Goddess actually forming the landscape, the stones which drop from her apron causing the hills and valleys, so we can see her in a sense giving birth to the landscape, and showing her aspect of Earth Goddess again.

"Determined now her tomb to build,
Her ample skirt with stones she filled,
And dropped a heap on Carron-more;
Then stepped one thousand yeards to Loar,
And dropped another goodly heap;
And then with one prodigious leap,
Gained carrion-beg; and on its height
Displayed the wonders of her might."[95]

In Scotland the Cailleach Bheur was said to have formed the hills of Ross-shire with earth and stones that fell off her back. Likewise she also dropped stones out of her pannier to form Ben Vaichaird.

"When standing on the site of the huge Ben Vaichaird, the bottom of the pannier is said to have given way, and the contents, falling through the opening, produced the hill, which owes its great height and vast extent of base to the accident."[96]

A Manx tale from the Isle of Man tells of how the Caillagh ny Gromagh fell into a crevice whilst trying to step from the top of Barrule to the top of Cronk yn Irree Lhaa, leaving the mark of her heel visible to this day.

---

[95] John Swift (1667-1745).
[96] *Scenes and Legends of the North of Scotland* – Hugh Miller, 1835, p30

Shaping the Land

Morrígan's Site Locations

There are a large number of places in Britain and Ireland that are specifically connected with the Morrígan or with one of more of her guises.

In addition to the sites listed below, it is interesting to note that a common name for megalithic tombs in Ireland is Diarmuid and Grainne's Bed, after the time they spent hiding for a year and a day whilst being pursued by Finn (see chapter 14 for more details of this story).[97] As will be discussed later, Grainne may also be seen as a guise of the Morrígan.

It is interesting to see that most of the sites associated with the Morrígan are either connected with water, or are hills or mountains. This reinforces her role as an Earth or Nature Goddess. Likewise, mounds in general, which were seen as entrances to the otherworld, were associated with her in her role as the Faery Queen.

England

Dane Hills

Black Annis' cave was located in the Dane Hills in Leicestershire, and is the centre of her myth, affecting all who lived within a substantial radius of the hills.

Isle of Man

Cronk yn Irree Lhaa

Cronk yn Irree Lhaa in the Isle of Man is said to be the home of the Caillagh ny Groamagh.

---

[97] *Sacred and Secular Neolithic Landscapes in Ireland* – Gabriel Cooney, in *Sacred Sites, Sacred Places*, 1994, p39.

Ireland

Armagh

Armagh is named after the Macha, as is recorded in the
Dindshenchas: *"And after this she died, and her tomb was raised on
Ard Macha, and her lamentation was made, and her gravestone was
planted. Whence Ard Machae, Macha's Height."*[98]

Banshee Sites

There are also sites in Ireland particularly linked with the banshee.
Rocks are sometimes associated with the banshee as her chair, upon
which she would mourn the coming death of a person in the
neighbourhood. Such rocks include *The Banshee's Chair* in
Modeligo, Waterford, *The Bow Stone* in Patrickswell, Carlow and
Corby Rock Mill in Monaghan.[99]

The banshee also sometimes turns up in urban areas as well as her
more usual rural setting. There is also a lane in Wexford known as
The Black Cow (note the cow association of the Morrígan).[100]

Bed of the Couple

The "Bed of the Daghda", the ford where the Daghda and Morrígan
were said to have united, also became known as the "Bed of the
Couple", and is located at the Dindgnai in Broga.

Búan's Well

Búan's Well in Iveragh, Co. Kerry, is named after the warrior woman
Búannan, who is a guise of the Morrígan.

---

[98] *Rennes Dindshenchas*, no. 94.
[99] *The Banshee: The Irish Death Messenger* – Patricia Lysaght, p126.
[100] *Ibid*, p127.

Ceann Bóirne

Ceann Bóirne on the peninsula in northwest Clare is another site linked to her through the *Brónach Bóirne* (brónach of Ceann Bóirne) or Hag of the Black Head.

Dá chích na Morrígna

The Dá chích na Morrígna or "Paps of the Morrígan" (recalling the Paps of Anu in Luchair) is located near Newgrange in Co. Meath.

Dorsey Ramparts

The Morrígan was supposed to have thrown a white stone from Slieve Gullion to the Dorsey Ramparts several kilometres away. The tradition of keeping the stone whitewashed is still observed annually.

Gort na Morrígna

Gort na Morrígna (the Morrígan's Field) in Co. Louth is another of her sites, and recalls the meanings of the name Macha.

Sliab na Caillighe

At Sliab na Caillighe there is a throne-shaped limestone boulder known as The Hag's Chair. Local tradition tells of how Cailleach Beara came down from the north to perform a magical task, by which she could gain great power.

She dropped her apronful of stones at the site, leaving them as it is today. It is interesting to note the apron as the symbol of the womb here, and the emphasis again on sovereignty of the land – the stones and the throne shape.

Slieve Gullion

The south cairn on Slieve Gullion was believed to be the entry to her womb, and to the Otherworld. With her connection to water, it is not surprising to note that there is a track from the cairn to a circular pool near by.

It was in this cairn that the hero Finn spent Midsummer night with her, and came out an old man (drained by her embrace), symbolising the beginning of the decline of the sun in its solar cycle, for Finn was very much the solar hero.

Tobar na Baidhbe

Tobar na Baidhbe (the Badhbh's Well) in Co. Waterford is another site associated with her, both as the Badb and also as the banshee.

Scotland

Beinn Chailleach Bheur

There is a hill called Beinn Chailleach Bheur in the parish of Strathlachlan and Strachur in Cowal, Argyllshire named after her.

Beinn na Caillich

A hill in Kidalton parish, Islay called Beinn na Caillich is named after her, and a furrow down its side called Sgrìoh na Caillich was said to be made by her as she slid down it in a sitting position.

Ben Cruachan

In Scotland the well on the summit of Ben Cruachan in Argyll is sacred to the Cailleach. Loch Awe was said to have been created by her as well (see chapter 3 *Wise Crone: Tales of the Cailleach*).

Ben Nevis

Ben Nevis, the tallest mountain in Scotland, was said to be the home of the Cailleach Bheur in the myths where she keep Princess Bride, the summer maiden, captive working on her winter mantle.

Corryvreckan

The whirlpool Corryvreckan, which lies between the northern end of Jura and the isle of Scarba in the Inner Hebrides, as well as being known as Coire-Bhrecain (the cauldron of Brecan) was also known as "The Morrígan's Cauldron".

Firth of Cromarty

The Firth of Cromarty on the Scottish coast was the home of the Cailleach in her form of Weather Goddess, where she was known as Gentle Annie and could bring storms at a moment's whim.

The Cooking Spit

The Morrígan is described as having a great magical cooking-spit at her dwelling. Her spit held three pieces of food at any given time – a piece of raw meat, a piece of dressed meat and a piece of butter. The raw meat would be dressed, the dressed meat never burned, and the butter never melted, even when it was in the fire.

There is a reference to her giving this spit to a group of thieves, who dismantle it and each carry a piece of the spit.[101] This is a curious fragment, and bears similarities to the Daghda's giant spit which cooked huge amounts of meat. It may hint at an earlier fertility connection, as the Morrígan and the Daghda are linked in a number of texts.

---

[101] *On the History and Antiquities of Tara Hill* – George Petrie, 1839, p213-4

6. The Faery Queen

"Behold the chariot of the Fairy Queen!
Celestial coursers paw the unyielding air;
Their filmy pennons at her word they furl,
And stop obedient to the reins of light;
These the Queen of Spells drew in;
She spread a charm around the spot,
And, leaning graceful from the ethereal car,
Long did she gaze, and silently,
Upon the slumbering maid."[102]

The Morrígan is associated with a whole host of faery beings across Britain and France. The best known of these faery occurrences of the Morrígan is the banshee in Irish folklore. The important consideration here is the word *sídh*, which is often associated with the Morrígan in her different guises in the various tales. It translates as "faery hill" or "faery mound", and indicates the connection between the Goddess and the faery folk.

Landscape features like mounds or burial chambers, and bodies of water, were considered to be entrances to the other worlds – faery realms of the land of the dead. Rivers, fords, lakes, springs, and wells all play an important part in Celtic myths, and we should also recall the Celtic habit of throwing votive offerings (which were usually carved and shaped to resemble body parts for healing, or broken weapons, tools or jewellery for propitiation of the Gods) into bodies of water.

As Ireland became more Christian, the old Gods lost their worshippers (at least publicly), and were either assimilated into the Christian pantheon as saints, such as the Goddess Bride or Brigid becoming St Brigid, or they were demonized into faery beings. From being the name for the pantheon, the term Túatha Dé Danann became a generic term for the faery folk.

That the Morrígan is seen as the Queen of the faery Túatha Dé Danann is an interesting survival of the fact that Danu is another guise of the complex Goddess that is the Morrígan.

---

[102] From *Queen Mab* - Percy Blythe Shelley (1792–1822).

Local folklore in Ireland has the Morrígan leading the Faery Court across the land at Samhain. This echoes practices across Britain and Europe of the Wild Hunt being led across the land at this time of year, e.g. Herne and the Wild Hunt around Windsor in England, Gwyn Ap Nudd and the Cwn Annwn (Hounds of the Underworld) in Wales, Dame Holda and the Wild Hunt in Germany and Odin in the Norse countries. The travelling faery group represents the powers of chaos being dominant at the time of darkness when the veil between the worlds is thinnest.

The whole of the conflict of the Táin is also linked to the Morrígan's role as Faery Queen of the folk and beings of the otherworld. For the two great bulls who are destined to fight, and who Queen Medb is determined to possess, have a history.

In *De Cophur in Dá Muccida* ("The Quarrel of the Two Pigkeepers")[103] we discover that the two great bulls are reincarnations of two swineherds to the fairy (*síd*) kings of Connacht and Munster. These two were originally friends but their masters were enemies, and they ended up becoming enemies as well.

As Faery Queen, by creating the situation where the two could fight again (as the bulls), the Morrígan brings an unresolved fairy feud into the mortal realm, which also has the added benefit of a huge amount of slaughter to keep her more bloodthirsty side happy.

The fact that there is more than one faery king is reminiscent of the husbands of Queen Medb. She has nine different husbands as well as numerous lovers. By human standards this may seem amoral, but the faery are a different type of being, and cannot be judged by the standards of human society.

The faery association with the long-haired banshee is evidenced by her frequent use of a comb.[104] The combing of the hair is frequently reported for sightings of the banshee, and indeed the comb is her prized possession. This is also the case for other magical beings associated with water, such as mermaids and nymphs.

In the case of men stealing her comb, they inevitably decide very quickly to return her comb, and if lucky may only receive an imprint on

---

[103] A foretale to the *Táin* itself.
[104] See e.g. *The Dead-Watchers and Other Folk-Lore Tales of Westmeath* – Patrick Barden, 1891, Mullingar, p82.

their skin from her immensely strong fingers. The extraordinary strength of the Banshee can be seen as another indication of her connection to the Morrígan.

It is interesting to note that one of the Welsh terms for the faery folk is *Bendith y Mamau*, meaning "the Mother's Blessing", as this recalls the meaning of Túatha Dé Danann ("Children of Danu"). As we have seen that Danu equates to the Morrígan, we can speculate on a link between the faery of Wales and of Ireland.

Baobhan Sith

A Scottish variant of the blood-drinking faery is the *Baobhan Sith* ("Faery Woman"). This word is the Highland equivalent of Banshee, though the Baobhan Sith is more of a Lamia by nature. They are a type of succubus that only come out at night and will drain a person of blood, but in classic faery fashion cannot stand iron.[105]

A story of the Baobhan Sith recounts their bloodthirsty nature.[106] Four young men on a hunting trip spend the night in an empty hut. They decide to amuse themselves and three of them start dancing, whilst the other one makes music. One of the men wishes that they had women to dance with, and immediately four women appear, and go to each of the men.

The music-maker notices drops of blood falling from his three friends, and runs away, pursued by the fourth Baobhan Sith. He hides amongst the horses, protected by the iron of their horseshoes, and the Baobhan Sith circles him all night, disappearing when the sun rises. When he returns to the hut he finds the bloodless corpses of his three friends, sucked dry by the Baobhan Sith.

---

[105] *Scottish Folk Lore and Folk Life* – Donald MacKenzie, 1935, p236.
[106] *Ibid.*

Faery Birds

The theme of faery birds occurs in *The Conception of Cú Chulainn (Compert Con Culainn)*. A flight of faery birds lay waste to the plain before Emain Macha, and are pursued by the druid Conchobar and his daughter (or in some versions wife) Deichtine.

"The flight of the birds, and their song, captivated the Ulstermen with their beauty. There were nine score birds in all, with a silver chain between each pair of birds, and each score flew its own way. And two birds flew out in front, a silver yoke between them."[107]

The birds eventually lead the party to a house where they feast, and the God Lugh appears to Deichtine in her dreams and tells her she will bear his child. Thus was the hero Cú Chulainn conceived.

A second version of the story has Deichtine and fifty maidens transformed into the faery birds. After three years of searching the men of Ulster find the maidens at a faery house, and Cú Chulainn is born there.

The theme of faery birds also occurs in *The Wasting Sickness of Cú Chulainn (Serglige Con Culainn)*. The men of Ulster and their wives have gathered at the Plain of Murthemne to celebrate Samhain, when a flock of beautiful birds land on a lake nearby.

All the women want a pair of the birds, but argue over who is worthy of owning them. Cú Chulainn catches them all and distributes them, but when he finishes giving them out he realises there are none left for his wife. (His wife is called Ethne in this text rather than her usual name of Emer.) She is angry at being left out and he promises her the next pair of birds to arrive.

A pair of birds joined together by a chain arrives.[108] Recognising their otherworldly nature (the connecting chain symbolises this); his wife and charioteer urge him not to use his sling on them. Cú Chulainn

---

[107] *Compert Con Culainn (The Conception of Cú Chulainn)*, from *The Book of Druimm Snechta*

[108] This motif of the two birds connected together with a chain occurs in a number of stories as a sign of the otherworld. See *The Dream of Oengus (Aislinge Oengusso)* and *The Conception of Cú Chulainn (Compert Con Culainn)*.

ignores them and on his third strike hits one of the birds on the wing. (Note the triple motif here again).

Cú Chulainn subsequently falls asleep sitting against a pillar stone and has a dream where two beautiful women laugh at him and beat him ferociously with a whip. When he wakes he is unable to speak and lies sick in bed for a year. Such is his punishment for attacking the faery women, after ignoring the omen of missing them twice when he threw the stones. The fact that he had never missed a throw in his life before should have made him realise that the misses were for a magical reason.

The magical, otherworldly nature of the women is subsequently revealed when Cú Chulainn is invited to the faery realms to fight for one of the women in battle, with the promise of her favour. He does so, but the subsequent tryst is prevented by his wife, who intervenes and holds his favour by strength of words and personality.

Faery Ravens

The tradition of three faery ravens also seems to have its roots in the powers and attributes of the Morrígan. In the tale of *Agallamh na Senórach* there are three faery ravens that come every Samhain (November 1st) to carry off three boys from a faery mound.

The three heroes of the story kill the three ravens by throwing chess pieces at them. This combination of ravens and chess is reminiscent of *The Dream of Rhonabwy* from *The Mabinogion*.

A fragment variant about Cú Chulainn has him killing a flock of malicious otherworldly ravens.[109] The ravens are described as being huge and capable of swimming on the waves of the sea, emphasising their faery nature. Cú Chulainn pursues them and kills the entire flock with his sling.

He performs a ritual with the last bird that emphasises his link to the Morrígan as a tutelary Goddess. He cuts off the dead bird's head and bathes his hands in the blood. This act is highly suggestive of both an attempt to gain the magical powers of the raven, and also an offering to the Morrígan. The rock he set the head on is then called *Srub Brain* ("Raven's Bill").

---

[109] *Rennes Dinschenchas.*

Glaistig

The *Glaistig* (alternative forms *glaistic, glaisnig, glaislig, glaisric* and *glaislid*) is a faery being who seems to have a lot in common with the Cailleach. Her name is suggested as meaning either *water imp* or *hag*, from *glas* meaning *water* and *stic* meaning *imp* (or *hag*).[110] She is described as being half-woman and half-goat, and to frequent lonely lakes and rivers, repeating the common water connection.

The Glaistig herself however takes credit for actions ascribed to the Cailleach Bheur, such as the heap of stones known as the Carn-na-Caillich. A Gaelic rhyme has her saying:

"Know ye the Cailleach's cairn
On that green hillside yonfer?
It was I that gathered it with a creel,
Every pebble that is in it,
To put a bridge on the Sound of Mull –
And to put it there were easy,
Had not the neck-rope broken,
It were there now beyond doubt."[111]

Her attributions are diverse and seem to have accreted a wide range of associations. She is variously depicted as being very tall or small. She is said to be able to change into a variety of animal forms, including dog, foal, mare and sheep, demonstrating the ability to shape-shift. She was said to enjoy herding sheep and cattle (like the Cailleach Bheur).

A variant of the Glaistig, known as the Gruagach, was described as having long golden hair and wearing a green dress. These are classic faery attributes, and the Gruagach could be either beautiful or wan and haggard. She would guard cattle, and always stayed close to water. At times she would visit houses and ask to come in and dry herself by the fire, as she would always be dripping wet.

Indeed it was believed that if offerings of milk were left out for her she would herd and look after cattle for people. She was also said to look

---

[110] Carmichael in *Carmina Gadelica* volume 2:287.
[111] Translation given in *Scottish Folk-Lore and Folk Life* – Donald MacKenzie, 1935, p177.

after lonely elderly people and people of simple mind, as well as enjoying playing games with children.

She was said to live either in a cave, or by water at fords or in a waterfall. She was also thought to wail to foretell deaths in old families, in a manner similar to the Banshee. She was usually considered invisible, but when she permitted herself to be seen she would be dressed in faery green, and then be known as *à Ghlaistig uaine* ("the green Glaistig").

As well as Banshee attributions she has also gained mermaid ones, like the Breton Morgen. She was described as having long golden hair, which she would be seen combing whilst stretched out on a rock. In this aspect she was known as the *gruagach mhara* ("sea-maid"), and was even known to become the familiar of pirates.

There were also malicious Glaistigs, who would attack travellers at fords. They would question the traveller first, and any weapon or item the traveller named he could not subsequently use to harm the Glaistig. A cunning traveller would thus only describe weapons and never name them.[112] These Glaistigs were considered to be members of the Fuath, the class of Scottish faeries associated with water and considered to be particularly dangerous to humans.

---

[112] This folklore on the Glaistig is drawn from chapter 9 *The Glaistig and Bride* of MacKenzie.

Leanan Sídhe

The *Leanan Sídhe* ("faery sweetheart" or "faery mistress") is another faery whose roots are to be found in the tales of the Morrígan. In Irish folklore, she is a dangerous poetic muse, providing those who follow her with a short but creative and glorious life.

The Leanan Sídhe would inspire her lover with creativity, but she also burned away his life-force, causing him to die young. Her influence can easily be imagined in the world of music, where many great performers die young.

"Most of the Gaelic poets, down to quite recent times, have had a Leanhaun Shee, for she gives inspiration to her slaves and is indeed the Gaelic muse -- this malignant fairy. Her lovers, the Gaelic poets, died young. She grew restless and carried them away to other worlds, for death does not destroy her power."[113]

There is also a Manx variant of this faery, found on the Isle of Man and called the Lhiannon-Shee. This variant is however more of a succubus, draining the life essence from her lovers.

---

[113] *Fairy and Folk Tales of Ireland* – W.B. Yeats, MacMillan, 1983.

Morgens

As is discussed in the next chapter, the name Morgan means, *"born of the sea"*. In Brittany this name seems to be the root of the Morgens, mermaids who have long golden hair and heavy fish-tales of grey-blue scales. They are said to be "born of the sea", and sit combing their long hair and luring unwary men to their underwater palaces in true mermaid style. Both the long hair and the comb are classic faery motifs, as has already been mentioned.

These Morgens, or Morganes, are said to come from the princess Morgane who caused the sinking of the city of Ys. The king's daughter was said to be lustful and take many lovers (in true Morrígan style), and because of her depravity the city was sunk.

It has been suggested that the malicious mermaid called Morgan in Wales is from the same source as the Morgens.[114] This Morgan was said to haunt Lake Glasfryn Uchaf in the parish of Llangybi, and come out of the lake to steal away naughty or over-adventurous children.

---

[114] *Celtic Folklore* – Rhys, 1:365-76.

Princess Mis

The transformations of the princess Mis are also worth detailing as they seem to describe a supernatural transformation with qualities of the faery Morrígan being gained.

Princess Mis goes searching for her father, who has been fighting in a battle. She finds her dead father's body and in her distress she drinks the blood from his wounds, which sends her mad.[115]

She subsequently flees to the mountains where her hair grows so long it reaches the ground and her nails become like claws (both faery motifs). She runs like the wind and catches wild animals, which she eats raw. She is eventually tamed by the harper Dub Ruis by means of his soothing music and sexual intercourse.

---

[115] *Scél Mis ocus Dub Ruisi* (The Romance of Mis and Dubh Ruis).

Queen Mab

"O, then, I see Queen Mab hath been with you.
She is the fairies' midwife, and she comes
In shape no bigger than an agate-stone
On the fore-finger of an alderman,"[116]

In Shakespeare the Faery Queen has been reduced to a tiny figure, belittling the power of otherworldly beings. It seems likely that Queen Medb of the Irish myths has become Queen Mab, but in a substantially reduced form.

Both characters share a number of characteristics that indicate this commonality. In addition to the similarity of their names, they are both fiercely independent queens, both highly sexual. In his speech in *Romeo and Juliet*, Mercutio makes a number of references which seem to substantiate the derivation of Mab from Medb, and hence ultimately the Morrígan.

The first obvious connection is the horse link, for Shakespeare says *"This is that very Mab that plats the manes of horses in the night."*[117] Even though she is very small, Mab is still given the appropriate means of travel, *"Her chariot is an empty hazel-nut."*[118] We may observe that although the chariot is small, still she rides it alone, in the manner of the Warrior Queen. The chariot is made from hazel, representing wisdom in the Celtic myths.

He also refers to her saying, *"This is the hag".*[119] This reminds us of the hag/maiden Bestower of Sovereignty found repeatedly in tales linked to the Morrígan.

The ability to influence dreams is another trait associated with the Morrígan, as when she sends the prophetic dream to the Fir Bolg King forewarning of his defeat.[120] Although Shakespeare refers to Mab's effects on all different sorts of dreamers, he does hint at the link by placing so much emphasis on the soldier's dream, i.e. the war

---

[116] *Romeo and Juliet* I:4 – William Shakespeare (1564-1616).
[117] *Romeo and Juliet* I:4.
[118] *Romeo and Juliet* I:4.
[119] *Romeo and Juliet* I:4.
[120] *Cath Muighe Tuireadh.*

connection that is entirely appropriate for a figure derived from the Morrígan:

"Sometime she driveth o'er a soldier's neck,
And then dreams he of cutting foreign throats,
Of breaches, ambuscadoes, Spanish blades,
Of healths five-fathom deep; and then anon
Drums in his ear, at which he starts and wakes,
And being thus frighted swears a prayer or two
And sleeps again."[121]

Ben Jonson continued the legend of Queen Mab, writing of her in his *Entertainment of the Queen and Prince at Althrope* in 1603:

"This is Mab, the mistress fairy,
That doth nightly rob the dairy,
And can hurt or help the churning,
(As she please) without discerning.
She that pinches country-wenches
If they rub not clean their benches,
And with sharper nails remembers
When they rake no up their embers;
But, if so they chance to feast her,
In a shoe she drops a tester.
This is she that empties cradles,
Takes out children, puts in ladles;
Trains forth midwives in their slumber,
With a sieve the holes to number;
And thus leads them from her boroughs,
Home through ponds and water-furrows.
She can start our franklin's daughters,
In their sleep, with shrieks and laughters,
And on sweet St. Agens' night
Feed them with a promised sight,
Some of husbands, some of lovers,
Which an empty dream discovers."

Jonson also refers to several of the associated qualities of the Faery folk, showing the common views of his time. Mab influences dreams, robs the dairy, pinches wenches and steals children.

---

[121] *Romeo and Juliet* I:4.

Tales of Thomas the Rhymer or True Thomas

Thomas the Rhymer, also known as True Tom, was a lover of the Faery Queen, who seems to have been based on a historical figure born in the early thirteenth century (Thomas of Erceldoune). He is of interest because he was given the gift of prophecy by the Faery Queen, and also in versions of the tale she herself made prophecies concerning the outcome of battles and claims to Sovereignty (both Morrígan characteristics). This includes the battle of Falkirk in 1298, the battle of Halidon Hill in 1333, the battle of Otterbourn in 1387, and Henry IV's invasion of Scotland in 1401.

In different versions of the myth Thomas stays with the Faery Queen for three or seven years, and is either given the gift of prophecy, or else given a cursed fruit to eat which prevents him from ever lying.

The description of the Faery Queen in the different versions usually has identifying faery motifs. In one version we find, *"in her hand she held bells nine;"*[122] giving the sacred nine, and also bells which are sacred to the faery. Another tale has her in the classic faery green: *"Her skirt was of the grass-green silk".*[123] In all cases she is riding a horse, showing the equine connection.

The journey to the otherworld is like a heroic epic, for it was long and involved much toil, and also contains more Morrígan symbolism, such as blood. Wading through red blood is strongly reminiscent of the Washer at the Ford.

"For forty days and forty nights
He wade thro red blade [blood] to the knee,
And he saw neither sun nor moon,
But heard the roaring of the sea."[124]

Several versions of the tale describes the faery Queen turning into a hag with blue skin ("bloo as beten led" – blue as beaten lead). This clearly recalls the blue-skinned hag guise of the Morrígan as the Cailleach and Black Annis.

---

[122] *MSS Campbell HISS II.83.*, see also *Lansdowne MSS 762, Ctton Vittell E* and *Thornton.*
[123] Jamieson's *Popular Ballads II.7* and *Minstrelsy of the Scottish Border II.251.*
[124] Jamieson's *Popular Ballads II.7.*

"Thomas stondand in that sted
And beheld that lady gay
hir here that hong vpon hir hed,
her een semyd out, that were so gray.
And alle hir [rich] clothis were Away.
that there before saw in that stede;
the toothe blak, the tothur gray,
the body bloo as beten led."[125]

This then continues with Thomas referring to her face having previously been as bright as the sun, recalling the Grian connection of the Morrígan, which is discussed in chapter 3 *Wise Crone: Tales of the Cailleach*, in the context of her relationship to the Cailleach in tales like *The Venomous Boar of Glen Glass*.

"that thou art so fadut in the face, that before schone as sunne bright."[126]

---

[125] *Cambridge University MS, p119.*
[126] *Cambridge University MS, p119.*

7. Liminal Goddess

A guise of the Morrígan that is often ignored is her role as a Liminal Goddess. Liminal deities are those who rule over changes of state, of transformation and boundaries. The Morrígan is associated with liminal states throughout the myths.

As the Washer at the Ford she is a liminal being, for the ford is the place where the land and the river meet. The ford is neither earth nor water, but partakes of both. Also the Washer at the Ford is predicting death, which is the ultimate transition.

The liminal time of the year is Samhain, the beginning of winter in the Celtic worldview, when the veil between life and death was seen as being the thinnest. This liminal time was linked to faery birds on two occasions in Celtic tales.

In *The Wasting Sickness of Cú Chulainn* (*Serglige Con Culainn*), the men and women of Ulster have gathered at the Plain of Murthemne to celebrate Samhain, when the flock of beautiful birds which precipitate the problems in the story landed on the nearby lake. In the tale of *Agallamh na Senórach*, three faery ravens came every Samhain to carry off three boys from a faery mound.

The Scottish Cailleach Bheur was seen as being either reborn at Samhain, or transforming from the Summer Queen to the Winter Queen. Samhain was also the time when the Morrígan led the faery court across the land.

The most liminal event in the Celtic myths occurs at Samhain. This is when the Morrígan has sex with the Daghda astride the ford, with a foot on each bank, before the Second Battle of Moytura.[127] Not only is it Samhain, but the sexual act takes place across the river, with a foot on each shore. This straddling of the water, representing the boundary or threshold to the Otherworld, at the liminal time of Samhain, is an extremely powerful symbolic act, representing the powers of life (sex) and death (battle).

The threshold is another liminal place. In the tale of *Da Derga's Hostel* we see great emphasis on the liminal. The hostel itself was said to exist on the boundary between the physical world and the

---

[127] *Cath Maige Tuired,* and also *Dindshenchas.*

Otherworld, and was itself a liminal place. When the Badb appeared to force King Connaire to break his geis, she stood on the threshold, doubly emphasizing the liminal nature of the encounter.

The Badb stood at the entrance in the posture called *corrguinecht*, a cursing posture which is in itself liminal, as it involves standing on the left leg and pointing with the left hand, with one eye closed. The Badb also recited a string of words, amongst which was the liminal word Samhain.

This liminal posture is also used by the Morrígan in the tale of *Bruiden Da Chocae*. In this story Cormac, the successor to the throne, is on his way to claim his crown. When he sees the Washer at the Ford and sends a man to speak to her, she assumes the *corrguinecht* posture to foretell Cormac's doom.

Apart from fords, which are liminal as boundaries between the elements, mountains and faery mounds are also seen as being liminal places. Mountains are liminal as the place where the earth meets the air at a very high point. Faery mounds are gateways between the physical world and the Otherworld. Both these types of place are particularly associated with the Morrígan, the former in her guise of Cailleach, and the latter in her guise of Faery Queen.

8. Lady of the Beasts

Another guise of the Morrígan that may not be as obvious at first glance is as Lady of the Beasts. The Morrígan shape-shifts into a variety of different animal forms – crow and raven being the most common, but also eel, heifer, and wolf. In the *Dindshenchas* she is described thus: *"The Daghda's wife found her; the shape-shifting Goddess."*[128]

As a crow, the Morrígan often spoke to issue warnings. She whispered warnings of his imminent danger from the forthcoming raid into the ear of Donn of Cúailnge (the Brown Bull of Ulster), which she had foreseen with her prophetic powers.[129] She also appears as a talking crow in both *Aided Conn Culainn* and *Táin Bó Regamna*.

In her guise of the Scottish Cailleach Bheur the avian connection is greatly emphasised. She is described as transforming into a number of other birds as well, these being heron, gull, cormorant and eagle in local tales.

As well as shape-shifting into animal forms, the Morrígan also has specific associations to animals, such as the horse. A number of horse Goddesses can be seen as guises of the Morrígan. We can see the equine connection in the story of *"Noínden Ulad 7 Emuin Macha"*, where as Macha she outruns the fastest horses.

The other Goddesses who can be identified as guises of the Morrígan, and who have equine connections, are the Irish Goddess Áine, who was also known as *Lair Derg* (red mare), the Gallic Goddess Cathobodua, who is depicted with the horse and the raven, the Welsh Horse Goddess Rhiannon and the Gallic Horse Goddess Epona.

The Morrígan keeps herds of animals in her different guises. As the Morrígan she has a herd of otherworldly magical cattle, and as Cailleach Bheur she has a herd of deer. As Mala Lia she has a herd of swine. In all of these instances she jealously protects her herd, as one would expect from an animal protectress. Of all the beasts, apart from the crow the cow does seem to be her favourite animal.

---

[128] *Dindshenchas.*
[129] *Táin Bó Cúailnge.*

The *Dindshenchas* relates that when a bull belonging to the mortal girl Odras mated with one of her herd, the Morrígan turned the girl into a river (again water as a magical symbol as it was seen by the Celts) in her fury, for one of her cows being tainted with mortal stock. Some sources suggest that this was a deliberate act by the Morrígan and she transformed Odras out of pure meanness.

The Morrígan was responsible for the *Cattle Raid of Cooley* by stealing an Otherworldly cow belonging to Nera and transferring it to the earthly world to mate with the Brown Bull,[130] the calf which was born of the union with Donn then subsequently challenging Findbennach (the White-horned Bull of Connacht) and initiating the problematic events.

She also takes the form of a hornless white red-eared heifer to attack Cú Chulainn during his battle with Lóch at a ford, and subsequently appears as an old woman leading a three-teated cow whose milk magically heals herself form the wounds inflicted by Cú Chulainn.

The eel connection is interesting, as it is the closest creature in appearance to the snake in Ireland, and may imply the transformative abilities associated with the snake. Also it is a water creature that can also function on land, emphasizing her connection to both the land and the water.

---

[130] *Echtra Nerai.*

9. The Bestower of Sovereignty

The Celts viewed the land as being female, and the sovereign responsibility of the Goddess in one of her guises. This is reflected in the tales of Queen Medb (a humanised Goddess) and her selection of a suitable partner to be the divine consort to the Goddess of the Land.

As the *"Great Queen"*, the Morrígan would on occasion appear in one of her forms and test the king or would-be king to determine his suitability to rule. The ancient idea of the "king and the land are one" is clearly expressed through this testing.

If the king accepts the Goddess and sees past the hideous physical appearance she assumes, to recognise her sovereignty of the land, which he holds through her grace, she transforms into the beautiful young Goddess and consecrates him as the rightful king.

A further possible meaning of the name Cailleach reinforces this motif. The word was used as a synonym for *ben*, which means *wife*. Hence we see such references as: *"himself and his caillech and his daughter"*.[131] So in this context the hag is also the land as wife, to which the rightful sovereign must be married, symbolised by the sexual union of the hieros gamos, or sacred marriage.

This theme is well illustrated in the 5th century story of *Niall of the Nine Hostages*.[132] Niall and his brothers are lost in a wood and are desperately thirsty. They come upon a crone (the Cailleach) guarding a well. The crone demands a kiss from anyone who wishes to drink from the well.

Niall's four brothers all refuse the crone's offer (we can see here the magical connotations of water and the well as symbolising the magic of the Otherworld). Niall however accepts the *"hideous shape, thin-shanked, grey-headed, bushy-browed"* figure, and *"around her he closed his arms ... he strained her to his breast and bosom, as though she were for ever his own spouse."*[133]

---

[131] *Esnada Tige Buchet,*
[132] From *Echtra Mac Echach Muigmeddóin* (The Adventure of the Sons of Eochaid Muigmedón).
[133] *Echtra Mac Echach Muigmeddóin.*

At this the crone transforms into the most beautiful maiden, described as *"the fairest in human form"*. On asking her name, Niall is told, *"I am Sovereignty"*.[134] Here the Goddess is giving the future king her divine blessing, through sexual union and the granting of water from the otherworldly well.

In this instance the Goddess also makes a prophecy, for she compares his reign allegorically to their embrace. She tells him his reign will be rough at the beginning, smooth in the middle and have a peaceful end.

The Adventure of Daire's Sons tells of the five Lughaids and also demonstrates the motif of the Cailleach who is sovereignty in disguise. The five men are caught in a snowstorm whilst hunting and seek shelter. They find a hut, but the hag inside demands that they sleep with her in exchange for shelter. Each brother refuses except for the last of the five, Lughaid Láigde.

"The hag entered the bed, and Lughaid followed her. It seemed to him that the radiance of her face was the sun rising in the month of May. A purple bordered gown she wore, and she had beautifully coloured hair. Her fragrance was likened to a fragrant herb-garden. Then he mingled in love with her. "Auspicious is thy journey," said she, "I am Sovereignty, and the kingship of Erin will be obtained by thee.""[135]

Another clear example of the bestowing of sovereignty is from the 11th century. Following the death of king Brian Bóru, the fairy queen Aoibheall (who has foretold his death in the manner of the banshee) then decides which of his sons should gain the sovereignty and become king.[136]

In contrast to Niall, King Connaire does not see past the hideous crone-like appearance of the Badbh, and initially adheres to his geis not to spend the night with any adult women under the same roof as him, refusing entry to the hostel he is in. She then curses him and he lets her in, breaking the last of his taboos, and is subsequently killed in the night by raiders, he having shown himself an unworthy king.

---

[134] *Echtra Mac Echach Muigmeddóin.*
[135] *Cóir Anmanni* (Fitness of Names).
[136] *Cogadh Gaedhel re Gallaibh.*

This tale of *Da Derga's Hostel* describes the actions of the Morrígan when she withdraws sovereignty.[137] King Connaire was staying at a hostel, which was on the threshold of this world and the Otherworld. On his way to the hostel events have forced Connaire to break all his gessa except one.

The Badbh arrives as a hideous, black, crow-like hag in triple form, bleeding and with a noose around her neck, as if in sacrifice. In other versions of the text she is described as a faery witch figure called Cailb.

Standing at the entrance she perched on one leg and used only one hand (the left side of the body - a symbolism indicating the Otherworld, and showing the meeting was taking place at the threshold to the Otherworld). Connaire was under a geis, or taboo, which prevented him spending the evening or night after sunset with a single woman, no matter her age.

Connaire asks the Badbh to reveal her identity, and she replies with a series of thirty-two words (including Samhain, Ugliness, Oblivion, Crime, Conflict, Fray, Crash, Noise, Amazement, Nemain and Badbh) and gestures with her left hand, whilst standing on her left leg and with only her left eye open, cursing him (this is a posture used for cursing in the Celtic world).

With the Badbh was a man, whose description of possessing *"one hand, one eye and one leg, with a roast pig on his back still squealing"*,[138] is that of the Lord of the Otherworld, with the magical pig that endlessly regenerated.

Having been shamed by the Badbh, he permits her to enter the hostel, breaking his geis. He then subsequently dies, killed by raiders in the night, having now broken the last of his unbroken geis.

As with Cú Chulainn, Connaire eventually died because the Goddess had withdrawn her favour and then endeavoured to force him to break his geis, in Connaire's case demonstrating his unworthiness to reign after he has made bad judgements.

---

[137] *Togail Bruidne Da Derga.*
[138] *Togail Bruidne Da Derga.*

Corrguinecht

In the tale of *Bruiden Da Chocae* the Morrígan refuses to bestow sovereignty, and appears again as Badb in this role. She appears both as the Washer at the Ford and also on the door of the hostel to repeat her prophecy. The description of the Badb herself is ominous and implies the forthcoming doom:

She was lame and blind in the left eye. She wore a threadbare nondescript cloak. Each of her joints from crown to the ground was as dark as the back of a beetle. Her filleted grey-haired mane fell over her shoulders.[139]

Finally, although it does not specifically refer to the Morrígan or her influence, there is another key instant where we feel her magic is implied in regard to sovereignty, and in this case its removal from an inappropriate monarch.

In the *First Battle of Moytura*, the Fir Bolg King Eochaid becomes incredibly thirsty at a key moment and leaves the battlefield with one hundred and fifty of his warriors. He is pursued by one hundred and fifty of the Túatha Dé Danann warriors, who eventually kill him.

The key element here is the incredible thirstiness that suddenly comes upon Eochaid. As has already been shown in this chapter, extreme thirstiness and perishing due to not being able to get water are themes linked with the Morrígan. The fact that it should result in Eochaid's death and thus ensure victory for the Túatha Dé Danann seems too coincidental to not be the influence of the Battle Goddess.

Considering other derivative Goddesses, it is clear that the Welsh Rhiannon is also a Sovereignty Goddess associated with the faery. In the tale *Pwyll Prince of Dyved*[140] her faery association is first indicated by her being initially seen on a mound (i.e. faery dwelling) and riding a pure white horse indicating her divine and regal status. Both these characteristics also associate her with the land.

Another association with the land is the bag she gives Pwyll that he fills with food but is never full. This is akin to the cornucopia or horn of plenty, but in reverse. After their union Rhiannon gives away a huge quantity of rich gifts to all who ask, indicating her bountiful nature.

---

[139] *Bruiden Da Chocae.*
[140] In *The Mabinogion.*

The Wedding of Sir Gawain and Dame Ragnell[141] continues the mythical theme of the hag/maiden Bestower of Sovereignty. In this story, King Arthur gets separated from his men whilst hunting. He encounters a knight called Gromer Somer Joure (*"Lord of the Summer Day"*), who claims that Arthur has given some of his lands to Gawain, and demands a fight. As the knight is fully armoured and Arthur has only a bow he tries to talk his way out of it.

In return for not killing him, Sir Gromer makes Arthur swear to return in a year with the answer to the question of what women most desire. Gawain subsequently realises something is wrong, and offers to help Arthur find the answer to the question.

At the end of the year Arthur returns to the forest of Inglewood where his troubles started. There he encounters the "loathly lady" who is Dame Ragnell, sister of Gromer Somer Joure. She is described thus:

"Her face seems almost like that of an animal, with a pushed-in nose and a few yellowing tusks for teeth. Her figure is twisted and deformed, with a hunched back and shoulders a yard broad. No tongue could tell the foulness of the lady."

However she speaks with a *"sweet and soft"* voice and knows exactly what Arthur is after. She offers the answer to the riddle in exchange for the hand of Sir Gawain, the most beautiful and noble of Arthur's knights (i.e. the worthy hero). Arthur returns to court and tells Gawain, who agrees to the marriage.

Arthur then returns to the wood and gets the answer from Dame Ragnell, who tells him the answer is sovereignty. Arthur continues to his meeting with Sir Gromer, and after leading him on gives him the correct answer. He then returns to court with Dame Ragnell, who though she is clad in the finest outfit, cannot hide her hideous appearance. However Dame Ragnell is indifferent to her appearance or how people view her.

After the wedding feast is over, Dame Ragnell and Sir Gawain retire to their chamber. When she asks Sir Gawain to come to bed, she also asks if he would have her be beautiful by day or by night. She prefers day and he night, but he chooses her preference, and as a result she is beautiful by both day and night.

---

[141] Anonymous, 14th century. This tale has a number of similarities to *Sir Gawain and the Green Knight*, as will be seen.

We see this theme surviving in popular literature throughout the fourteenth century and into the fifteenth century, occurring in a number of tales. As well as the tales discussed the theme of the transformed loathly lady also occurs in *The Marriage of Sir Gawain*, *The Ballad of King Henry*, *The Ballad of Kemp Owyne* and *The Ballad of the Knight and the Shepherd's Daughter*.

Chaucer covered this theme in *The Wife of Bath's Tale*.[142] An unnamed knight of King Arthur's court rapes a maiden and is condemned to die, but Guinevere intervenes and sets him a question that he has a year and a day to find the answer to.

The question is *"what is it that women most desire?"* The knight searches high and low for the answer to no avail. On the way to the court at the end of the year he rides through a forest and sees twenty-four women dancing. Eager to ask them the knight approaches, for them all to vanish and leave an ugly hag to answer him.

The hag tells him the answer on condition that he will grant her request when she makes it. At King Arthur's court the knight boldly steps forward and gives the answer:

"My lige lady, generally, quod he,
Wommen desire to have sovereintee
As well over hir housbond as hir love,
And for to have been in maistrie him above."[143]

He is agreed to have answered correctly, but then the hag makes her request, which is that he marry her. She could not be persuaded otherwise, so the knight agrees, but then on the wedding night she chastises the knight for ignoring her.

She tells him to choose if he would like her to be old and ugly yet gentle and loving, or beautiful and young but false and unfaithful. The knight gives her the choice, handing the mastery to her. She then transforms to be beautiful and loving, giving him the best of both options because he surrendered sovereignty instead of trying to be superior.

---

[142] Lines 862-1270 of *The Wife of Bath's Tale*, in *The Canterbury Tales* – Geoffrey Chaucer (1342-1400).
[143] *The Wife of Bath's Tale.*

The *Tale of Florent*[144] is extremely similar to *The Wedding of Sir Gawain and Dame Ragnell* and *The Wife of Bath's Tale*, and was written by a contemporary and friend of Chaucer. It was published before Chaucer in 1483, and as there is no evidence of either of them plagiarizing each other it seems likely they were both recording a popular recurrent theme.

In the story Florent is the nephew of the Emperor, who has slain a man called Branchus. Branchus' grandmother gives him a *"day and tyme"* to answer the question of what women desire most or be killed.

Florent subsequently meets a hag under a tree, and she offers to tell him the correct answer if he will promise to marry her. Florent agrees and when he is summoned to answer, after giving many incorrect answers of his own, he gives the hag's correct answer and is spared.

Florent then weds the hag in secret. When they are in bed he turns his back to her, only to turn to her when he sees the chamber is full of light. She has transformed and is now fair and young. The transformed maiden gives him the choice of whether to have her fair by day and foul by night, or vice-versa.

He gives her the choice, yielding to her will, and she declares that she will always be fair unto death. She reveals her wicked stepmother had enchanted her to be a hag until she could win the love of and sovereignty over a noble knight.

A tale from the West Highlands called *Nighean Righ fo Thuinn* (*"The Daughter of the King under the Waves"*) also contains elements that show it is a survival of the Bestower of Sovereignty tale.[145] A loathsome hag turns up on the doorstep of the house of the Feen brothers begging a place to warm herself by the fire.

The two older brothers, Fionn and Oisin refuse her, but the third, Diarmaid, pleads that she should be allowed to warm herself. She creeps into his bed and he puts a fold of blanket between them. After a while he discovers to his amazement that she has changed into the most beautiful woman he has ever seen.

---

[144] *Tale of Florent*, from *The Confessio Amantis* - John Gower (1325-1408).
[145] *Popular Tales of the West Highlands* (Volume 3) – J.F. Campbell, 1892.

The refusal by the older brothers, followed by the acceptance of the youngest brother is a classic motif of the sovereignty bestowal, (such as in the aforementioned *Niall of the Nine Hostages* and *Adventures of Daire's Sons*) as is the transformation into beautiful woman from loathsome hag.

A final tale worth mentioning is from Iceland, *The Saga of King Hrolf Kraki*,[146] showing a crossover into the Norse mythos. King Helgi is trying to sleep in his hunting lodge in the forest during the freezing cold of winter. Just as he is getting to sleep a scratch and a moan come from the door.

He opens the door to an ugly, thin hag wearing only a single ragged garment, who asks for shelter from the bitter cold of the elements. Helgi gives her a bear hide to wrap herself in and tells her to sleep on the floor.

The hag initially cajoles and then demands her way into his bed, to sleep under the blankets. As soon as he touches her she becomes young and beautiful. She then subsequently bears him a daughter called Skuld. It is worth noting that this is also the name of one of the Norns, the triple weavers of fate in the Norse myths, implying the sovereignty motif through control of fate.

---

[146] Recorded 1400, but may be much earlier.

Ériu as Sovereignty

"Ériu, though it should reach a road-end. Banba, Fotla and Fea, Neman of prophetic stanzas, Danu, mother of the Gods. Badb and Macha, greatness of wealth, Morrígan – source of enchantments, servants in her attendance, were the daughters of Ernmas."[147]

Together with her sisters Banba and Fotla, Ériu represented the sovereignty of Ireland, once again showing the triple motif associated with the Morrígan. The kings of Ireland wed the sisters to ensure their role as sovereigns.

"The three sons of Cermad son of The Dagda were Mac Cuill, Mac Cecht, Mac Griene: Sethor and Tethor and Cethor were their names. Fotla and Banba and Ériu were their three wives."[148]

One description of the goddess Ériu emphasises her connection to the Morrígan. She is described as alternating in appearance between being a beautiful woman one moment, and the next moment a grey-white crow.[149] This clearly links her to the Morrígan.

When the Milesians invade Ireland, they meet Ériu at Usnech of Mide. She welcomes them and praises them, telling them that the land will be theirs forever. Even though the Milesians defeat the Túatha Dé Danann, it is not an easy victory, and the Túatha Dé Danann gain the otherworld, Tir-na-Nog (*"The Land of Youth"*), the faery realm of Ireland which is said to exist under Ireland.

Ériu cleverly asks the Milesians to name Ireland after her, and to this day it still bears her name as Eire.

"It is naught to thee," said Ériu; "thou shalt have no gain of this island nor will thy children. A gift to me, O sons of Mil and the children of Bregan, that my name may be upon this island!"

"It will be its chief name for ever," said Amergin, "namely Ériu (Erin)."[150]

---

[147] *The Book of Invasions.*
[148] *The Book of Invasions.*
[149] *Battle of Tailtiu.*
[150] *The Book of Invasions.*

During the battle the Milesians kill Ériu, her sisters and their husbands, demonstrating that they will now have sovereignty over the land. However the Túatha Dé Danann get the better deal by claiming Tir-na-Nog as their own.

It is also clear that the land cannot die, and so neither really can sovereignty. Hence at the end of the battle with the Milesians, after the various deaths of Túatha Dé Danann heroes by the Milesian heroes have been recounted, we see:

"Ériu yonder, at the hands of Suirge
thereafter: Mac Greine of Amorgen.

Fotla at the hands of Etan with pride,
Of Caicher, Banba with victory,
Whatever the place wherein they sleep,
Those are the deaths of the warriors; hear ye."[151]

The key line is *"wherein they sleep"*, implying that the sovereignty embodied by Ériu is not destroyed, but recovering from the latest invasion.

---

[151] *The Book of Invasions.*

10. The Lover

The Morrígan is popularly perceived as a Goddess of Sex due to her coupling with the Daghda. Before the Second Battle of Moytura,[152] the Morrígan makes love with the Daghda astride a stream at Samhain, the time of the dead and ancestors. This union is detailed in the 12th century *Dindshenchas*.

"He [the Daghda] beheld the woman at Unius in Corann, washing herself, with one of her two feet at Allod Echae, to the south of the water, and the other at Loscuinn, to the north of the water. Nine loosened tresses were on her head. The Daghda conversed with her, and they made a union. 'The Bed of the Couple' is the name of the place thenceforward. The woman that is here mentioned is the Morrigu."[153]

This polarity of the fertility and life-symbolising Daghda with the dark and bloody Morrígan also emphasises the recognition of the continuity in change which comprises the cycle of life, and may be seen as the hieros gamos or sacred marriage for the continued well-being and fecundity of the land.

It also demonstrates a cultural example acknowledging the connection between sex and death (the Thanatos / Eros principle) as the Morrígan was fulfilling her role of Washer at the Ford foretelling death when the Daghda came upon her, and it was Samhain, the time of death and the ancestors.

The union taking place over a river also emphasises the magical nature of this union, as the Celts were aware of the sacred nature of water and its role as a boundary marker between realms; indeed in this instance the water may have symbolised the veil between life and death which is thinnest at this time, and which the two deities represent.

Some sources go so far as to refer to the Morrígan as the wife of the Daghda, such as *The Dindshenchas*, which says *"The Daghda's wife found her; the shape-shifting Goddess."*

---

[152] *Cath Maige Tuired*
[153] *Dindshenchas.*

In another tale the Daghda desires Boann (a guise of the Morrígan), and sends her husband Elcmar on an errand. He makes love with Boann, but he also stops the sun, so that nine months pass for them and she is able to give birth to Angus Og, whilst for Elcmar only one day passes and he is thus tricked into not knowing what has occurred.

Morrígan is identified in several of her guises as the wife of Néit (the God of Battle), including another name which suggests yet another guise for this complex Goddess. The name Fea is given as the wife of Néit as well as Morrígan, Macha, Nemain and Badb.

In the *"Founding of Emain Macha"*, she is desirable even though she is disguised as a leper. The five sons of Dithorba all try in turn to make sexual advances to her, and she overpowers all of them and forces them to build her fortress for her.

An important reference in the *Book of Lecan* lists sons attributed earlier in the *Cath Maige Tuired* to Danu, calling them sons of the Morrígan. It also directly links her to Danu and the term Túatha Dé Danann:

"The Morrígan ... was the mother of ... Brian, Iucharba, and Iuchair; and it is from her other name "Danu" the Paps of Ana in Luchair are named, as well as the Túatha Dé Danann."[154]

As well as these three sons, the tales in the *Book of Lecan* also mention her son Mechi, who was killed by Mac Cecht at Magh Fertaige, which was subsequently called *Magh Mechi*. Mechi had three serpents in his three hearts, which would have desolated all of Ireland if they had been allowed to grow.

As the version of Macha who dies on the finishing line of the Ulster horse-race and curses the Ulstermen, she bears twins called Fír (law) and Fial (principle). Both these names suggest her divine status as an Earth Goddess, implying order and the natural sequence of the cycles found in nature.

Queen Medb, who we may see as another guise of the Morrígan, was well known for her prodigious sexual appetites. She is recorded as having nine husbands, concurrently. Additionally we know from the tales that she also took numerous lovers, so that there was always

---

[154] *Book of Lecan.*

another one waiting to pleasure her as soon as the current one had left.

Medb does not hesitate to offer her sexual favours to gain whatever she wants (and also offers her daughter Findobair, who may be seen as an extension of her in the tales). In this manner she encourages the heroes Lóch mac Mo-Femis, Fergus and Fer Diad to fight for her. We may also note that Fergus, himself a major heroic figure, normally requires thirty women to satisfy him sexually, but Medb is fully capable of sating him.

Another child associated with the Goddess is the Faery King himself. Oberon is called the child of Morgan Le Fay and Julius Caesar in the early thirteenth century French tale of *Huon of Bordeaux*.

11. The Witch Goddess

One of the translations of the name Morrígan is "Witch Queen", and throughout the tales where she appears, reference is often made directly or indirectly to her magical abilities. If we consider these we see a number of different abilities demonstrated.

The first of these abilities is her frequent shape-shifting. The Morrígan demonstrates the ability to shift into all sorts of animal forms, and also appears in different humanoid forms, from maiden through to crone. The ability to assume other forms is one of the powers most associated with witchcraft.

"Morrígan – source of enchantments."[155]

Some of her actions demonstrate very powerful magic, and it is interesting to see that these are usually associated with the elements. Against the Fir Bolgs she brings down fire from the heavens, and when she is angry she transforms Odras into water.

One of the most common talents displayed by the Morrígan is that of prophecy. She does this at a number of key points, and by giving awareness of events to come she shows the ability to read the future, a skill that has always been in demand from witches, shamans and priestesses.

The Morrígan's use of the geis, or stricture, can be seen in a similar vein to the witch's curse. By laying a geis on a character, the Morrígan is essentially forcing them to behave in a certain way, and usually laying the grounds for their downfall later. Of course she also curses people on occasion as well, using the posture called *corrguinecht*.

---

[155] *The Book of Invasions.*

Shape-shifter

"The Daghda's wife found her; the shape-shifting Goddess."[156]

In a variety of tales the Morrígan shape-shifts to different human and animal forms – maiden, mature woman and crone, crow and raven (the most common), eel, heifer, wolf.

It has been observed that shape-changing and sexuality are convergent in some mythic cycles, and this is certainly true of the Morrígan. She appeared to Cú Chulainn as a beautiful young woman to try and seduce him when he was preparing for battle, but he spurned her saying he had more important things to do than have sex. Subsequently she appears as a hag, having been spurned as a maiden.

She then attacked him while he was fighting a human opponent, Lóch, at a ford, in the forms of an eel, grey-red wolf and hornless white red-eared heifer (both sets of colours indicating their magical otherworldly nature), incapacitating him each time so Lóch could wound him.

She was also wounded by him however, and then appeared to him as an old woman with a cow with three teats. He blessed her and she gave him milk, which restored his wounds, and then her wounds were also restored. The interconnectedness of the two and their mutual wounding and healing implies earlier layers to this story that we can guess at.

After his final battle when he has tied himself to a tree so as to die upright with honour, the Morrígan perches triumphantly on Cú Chulainn's dying body as a hooded crow, letting his enemies know it is safe to approach, but also guarding his body, reminding us she always wins in the end.

She also changes into differing ages – a young woman, a beautiful mature woman, and a hideous old hag, which is the classic triple Goddess image and also implies her sovereignty of the land.

We can see another derivative link that has interesting ramifications. It was a common belief about banshees that they could transform

---

[156] *Dindshenchas.*

themselves into hares.[157] However it as also a superstition across Ireland that hags transformed themselves into hares to suck milk from their neighbour's cows.[158]

The connection between hares and the goddess Andraste is discussed elsewhere, but further emphasises the connection of this animal with the Morrígan.

This belief also occurs in Scandinavia[159] and may indicate another migration of symbolism, as we see in a number of cases. It is significant that the shape-shifter is always an old woman, who may be injured by silver (the faery metal) when in hare form. This clearly hints at the survival of an older belief and connection to the Cailleach.

The transformation of witches into hares is well known in Scottish folklore, as in the trial of Isobel Gowdie in 1662, where she recounted the famous charm:

"I sall goe intill ane haire, With sorrow, and sych, and meikle care, And I sall goe in the Divellis nam, Ay whill I com hom againe."

The charm was sometimes varied by replacing the word *haire* (hare) with *blak thraw* (crow), a substitution which further links this connection back to the guises of the Morrígan.

A final literary reference to shape-shifting is that of Morgan Le Fay in *Le Morte D'Arthur*, when she is escaping from Arthur, where she transforms herself and her party into standing stones. This instance has been given as the basis for a number of stone circles around the British Isles such as the "Nine Maidens".

---

[157] *The Banshee: The Irish Death Messenger* – Patricia Lysaght, 1986, p109
[158] See *A Handbook of Irish Folklore* – S. Ó Súilleabháin, 1942, p33, 337; *The Old Woman as Hare: Structure and Meaning in an Irish Legend* – E. Ní Dhuibhne, 1993, in *Folklore* 104:77-85.
[159] See *The Witch as Hare or the Witch's Hare: Popular Legends and Beliefs in Nordic Tradition* – B. Nildin-Wall and J. Wall, Folklore 104:67, 1993, for more on the Nordic tradition of the milk-hare.

Vanishing

The Morrígan also makes things appear and disappear, e.g. her chariot and horse disappearing when she first meets Cú Chulainn, and the magical cow whose milk heals him after she has fought him in animal form.

Giants

The Irish sagas represent divinity by giant size on a number of occasions,[160] and it is significant to note that out of the descriptions of the deities given in *The Second Battle of Moytura*, only the Morrígan and the Daghda are described as being gigantic – for she stands with a foot on either side of the river and he has a club so big that its track is big enough for a boundary ditch.

Considering our earlier discussion of the Morrígan as being the daughter of Balor, we may also note with interest that he was also said to be gigantic, as it took a number of men to push open his eyelid to reveal his destructive eye.

The Cailleach is also gigantic on occasion by implication. To carry around boulders which form the landscape, as described for both the Irish Cailleach Bearra and the Scottish Cailleach Bheur, implies a gigantic figure.

In other texts Macha Mongruad is implied as being gigantic by her use of her brooch to measure out the site of Emain Macha. Queen Medb also has this giant size implied with her prodigious feats of urination, creating lakes and gullies with her urine.

---

[160] *The Mythology of All Races* – J.A. MacCulloch, 1918, *Celtic* 3:30.

Magical Use of Words

As has already been discussed the Morrígan uses words in a prophetic manner on a regular basis, both as the Washer at the Ford and also in victory prophecies or predictions of events to come (such as in her guises of Fedelm and Scáthach). She also predicts events when in crow form, such as when she warns the Brown Bull of the attempt to kidnap him.

The Morrígan also uses her poetry to riddle and confound, as when she encounters Cú Chulainn in the *Táin Bó Regamna*. The other form of words that she uses is cursing. In this context a geis could be seen as a form of curse, and so can her prophecies when she does not get what she wants.

The most famous curse she performs is the one issued by Macha as she lies dying after having given birth to twins at the end of the horse-race she has just won. She curses the men of Ulster:

"From this hour the ignominy that you have inflicted upon me will rebound to the shame of each one of you. When a time of oppression falls upon you, each one of you who dwells in this province will be overcome with weakness, as the weakness of a woman in child-birth, and this will remain upon you for five days and four nights; to the ninth generation it shall be so."

A magical posture used by the Morrígan on more than one occasion is the *corrguinecht*, (from the Gaelic *corrguine* meaning *magician* or *sorceror*) where only one arm, leg and eye are used. Hence the description from *Da Derga's Hostel* of the Badb standing on her left leg and pointing with her left hand and with one eye closed.

Of course words can also be used to manipulate without putting any magic beyond cunning into them. This is demonstrated by Queen Medb when she goads the hero Lóch mac Mo-Femis into fighting Cú Chulainn: *"You well deserve to be laughed at when the man who killed your brother is destroying our army without your going to fight him."*[161]

---

[161] *Táin Bó Cúailnge.*

The Geis

The *geis*, or *ges* as it is written in Irish, means "taboo" or "prohibited". A geis (pl. *gessa*) can only be laid by a woman, and the use of this magical stricture and the effects of it being broken are major themes throughout the Irish myths.

The definition of geis is:

> "A taboo, a prohibition, the infraction of which involved disastrous consequences ... such taboos might be attached to a rank or office ... They might bind a whole community ... more often they were restrictions on an individual, either owing to the predictions of druids or soothsayers that certain actions would bring ill-luck, or imposed on him by another who had power to punish their violation or who trusted to his sense of honour or his fear."[162]

The geis seems to have been mandatory for kings and heroes, and provides a way for the deities or faery to get rid of someone if they start to prove less than worthy, by making them break their gessa through cunning manipulation of events and people.

---

[162] *DIL*, p56-8.

Magical Warfare

The Morrígan demonstrates her magical ability in an aggressive manner in a number of ways. As Nemain, her shrieks can kill, as with the warriors at the battle of Connacht.

"Nemain, the war Goddess, brought confusion on the host ... so that a hundred warriors of them fell dead that night of terror"[163]

She speaks spells and transforms Odras into a river while she sleeps. The ability to transform the shape of others into water is reminiscent of the Greek Hunting Goddess Artemis, who also transformed those who annoyed her into pools and bodies of water.

When the first attack in the conflict against the Fir Bolg is carried out by the Morrígan, Badb and Macha, they bring down *"enchanted showers of sorcery and mighty showers of fire, and a downpour of red blood upon the warrior's heads, preventing them from moving for three days and nights."*[164]

The fixing of pillars in the ground to prevent anyone fleeing the battlefield could also imply some sort of spell. Even if the pillars act as a marker beyond which retreat was not allowed, they are still a form of magic in that none would dare retreat past them.

"The three sorceresses, Badb, Macha and Morrígan; Bé Chuille and Danu, their two foster-mothers. They fixed their pillars in the ground lest anyone flee before the stones should flee."[165]

---

[163] *Táin Bó Cúailnge.*
[164] *Cath Muighe Tuireadh.*
[165] *Cath Muighe Tuireadh.*

Numbers of the Morrígan

Throughout the tales there are two numbers commonly associated with the Morrígan. These are three and nine. Three was a particularly sacred number to the Celts, as was nine as three times three. Thus the symbolism of both these is found repeatedly through the myths.

Three

"The three sorceresses, Badb, Macha and Morrígan."[166]

"One of the three Morrígna, that is Macha and Badb and Morrígan."[167]

The Morrígan will often appear in three forms. With Badb and Macha she magically attacks the Fir Bolgs and prevents them from leaving Tara hill for three days and three nights.

Lugh is equipped with special weapons made for him by the "three Gods of Danu", Brian, Luchar and Lucharba, who are also called sons of the Morrígan.

Macha appears as three different manifestations through the Irish tales, as the Prophetess wife of Nemedh, as the wife of Crunnchu, and as Macha Mongruad, the warrior queen.

She appears as three Badbs in the tale of *Da Derga's Hostel*, when she stands on the threshold and forces king Connaire to break his geis.

When Cú Chulainn goes to study with Scáthach, her daughter Úathach tells him after three days the three demands he must make of Scáthach in order to study with her.

She attacks Cú Chulainn in three different animal forms and is wounded three times. As an eel she wraps herself around his legs three times. She then gives him three drinks of milk to heal the wounds. Ultimately three Badbs bring about his downfall.

---

[166] *Cath Muighe Tuireadh.*
[167] *Trinity H.3.18*

Nine

When the Daghda comes upon the Morrígan at the ford, she has nine braids in her hair.

Queen Medb is associated with the number nine, as she has nine husbands, and is always accompanied by nine chariots.

The ces noinden curse lasts for five days and four nights, a total of nine time periods, and affects the men of Ulster for nine generations. At the end of her Victory Prophecy the last line uttered by the Morrígan is *"peace to sky be this nine times eternal"*.

The wood hazel is referred to several times in connection with the Morrígan, and hazel is the ninth tree in the Ogham alphabet.

These numerical symbolisms are carried over into the various threads of the Arthurian mythos. E.g. in *Vita Merlini*, Morgan is the eldest of nine sisters; in *Le Morte D'Arthur*, there are three Queens in the boat that takes the mortally wounded Arthur to Avalon.

12. The Washer at the Ford

"Alas, the moon should ever beam
To show what man should never see!
I saw a maiden on a stream,
And fair was she!"[168]

Seeing the Morrígan as the Washer at the Ford was to have your (usually imminent) death foretold. In this respect she is a Goddess of Fate, for she is the one who cuts the thread of life, and determines the outcome of events. In this guise she appeared either as a beautiful maiden or as a hideous hag.

As previously mentioned, Cú Chulainn encountered her in this guise shortly before his death. She was often depicted in red, the blood red of the clothes she was washing the death stains from, though she would also be seen washing the armour and weapons as well, emphasising the violent end the warrior would be coming to.

"Here and there around us are many bloody spoils; horrible are the huge entrails the Morrígan washes. She has come to us, an evil visitor; it is she who incites us. Many are the spoils she washes, horrible the hateful laugh she laughs. She has tossed her mane over her back; a good, just heart hates her. Though she is near us, do not let fear startle you."[169]

In this guise she would predict which side would win in forthcoming battles, indicating an oracular aspect to her nature. It was as the Washer at the Ford that the Morrígan has sex with the Daghda,[170] also emphasising the connection of sex with the union of life and death.

In *Bruiden Da Chocae* the Washer at the Ford is the Badb guise of the Goddess. She foretells the death of Cormac in his unsuccessful bid for the kingship of Ulster. The Badb says, *"These are your own spoils, Cormac, and the spoils of favourites."*[171]

---

[168] *The Water Lady* – Thomas Hood (1799-1845).
[169] *Reicne Fothaid Canainne.* 9th-10th century.
[170] *Cath Maige Tuired.*
[171] *Bruiden Da Chocae.*

It is interesting to note that in this account the magical ability of the Badb is emphasised: *"They saw a red woman on the edge of the ford … when she put down her hand, the current of the river became red with blood and gore."*[172]

Initially Cormac sends one of his men to speak to her and find out what she is doing, and the Badb assumes the classic *corrguinecht* posture of the otherworld: *"And then she sang to him upon one foot and with one eye closed."*[173]

The last of the main Irish literary descriptions of the Washer at the Ford appears in the late 15th century in *Caithréimm Thoirdhealbhaigh*.[174] The descriptions in this are extremely detailed. Two battles are referred to; the first is the Battle of Corcomroe Abbey in North Clare on 15th August 1317, where she warns Donnchadh O'Brien of his imminent death.

This Washer figure is referred to as a Badb, and called the *Brónach Bóirne* (brónach of Ceann Bóirne) or Hag of the Black Head, referring to a peninsula in northwest Clare.

The description of the Badb given here is interesting, as it is very reminiscent of both Black Annis and one of the Scottish variants of the Cailleach. As this may indicate a commonality between these different aspects it is worth reproducing here:

"Over the shore of the bright lake rose a long great, stooped, blue-faced, wretched, hunchbacked, grey-toothed, coarse-furred, crook-nailed, tall, lean, red hag. The appearance of that spectral, squinting, watery-eyed, crooked, bent-shanked creature was like this: she had shaggy, rough-stranded, garlanded hair rough as heather, red and grey, which resembled seaweed."[175]

In the period before the second battle, Dysert O'Dea in May 1318, she warns the villainous Norman leader Richard de Clare of his forthcoming death, but he dismisses her as being in league with his enemies. He dies shortly after the second warning is given.

---

[172] *Bruiden Da Chocae.*
[173] *Bruiden Da Chocae.*
[174] *Caithréimm Thoirdhealbhaigh* (The Triumphs of Turlough) – John Mac Rory Magrath, 1495.
[175] *Caithréimm Thoirdhealbhaigh.*

The Washer at the Ford

A later appearance of the Washer at the Ford occurs in 1691 prior to the Battle of Aughrim. The Earl of Clanricarde of Tirellan castle and his servant come across a loud lamenting woman at a bog hole, who foretells the violent death of the Earl and Burke leading the Jacobite army.[176] That this should occur at the end of the seventeenth century is testimony to the enduring nature of the Goddess.

As time passed the Washer at the Ford became seen less as a Goddess and more as a faery, and in some instances even became downgraded to a mortal serving penance for sins or carelessness. The latter instance seems to be an attempt by the Christian church to both belittle these characters and also control their worshippers.

---

[176] *Scéaltaí Tíre: Bailiúchán Seanchais ó Ghaillimh.*

The Banshee – A survival of the Morrígan in folklore

"In her home, with bent head, homeless,
Clasping her knees she sits,
Keening, keening!
And at her keen the fairy-grass
Trembles on dun and barrow;
Around the foot of her ancient crosses
The grave-grass shakes and the nettle swings;
In haunted glens the meadow-sweet
Flings to the night wind
Her mystic mournful perfume;
The sad spearmint by holy wells
Breathes melancholy balm."[177]

Whilst the strong and feisty nature of the Morrígan ensured she would not be incorporated into Christianity as a saint, like other deities such as Bride; she nevertheless made the more gentle translation into folklore as the banshee or bean sí. This attribution is made clear by the names and attributions associated with the banshee.

This transition may largely be due to the incompatibility of the Morrígan with Christianity. In her comprehensive work *The Banshee*, Patricia Lysaght notes, *"Although certain Christian ideas and concepts enter into the death-messenger complex, it is in the main surprisingly a-Christian."*[178]

Some evidence does suggest though that the concept of the banshee existed by the eighth century. The Annals of Ulster for 737 record: *"Cernach son of Fogartach is treacherously slain by his wicked companions; the calves of cows and the women of the lowest world wearisomely lamented him."*

This intriguing entry gives a historical figure associated with mythical beings, for the lowest world is a reference to the faery realms, and the

---

[177] From *The Banshee* by John Todhunter (1839-1916).
[178] *The Banshee: The Irish Death Messenger* – Patricia Lysaght, p47.

lamenting suggests the banshee, although the banshee normally foretold death rather than lamenting afterwards.[179]

Across Ireland there are three main names associated with the banshee. These are bean sí, bean chaointe and badhbh. Let us consider these three terms in turn. Bean sí translates literally as *faery woman*, bean chaointe as *keening woman*, and badhbh as has already been stated means *scald crow*.

All of these names are obviously linked with the Morrígan, in her role as Faery Queen, her role as the Washer at the Ford, and in her guise of Badhbh. Hence we see *"Badhbh: a female fairy or phantom, said to be attached to certain families, appearing as a scald-crow or Royston-crow."*[180]

Banshees are usually described as being hideously ugly old hags (like some of the descriptions of Badb) or beautiful women with long golden hair and white dresses. This is a classic faery description recalling the Morrígan as Faery Queen. Whether ugly or beautiful her hair is usually described as being anything from waist-length to so long that it reaches the ground.[181]

It is recorded as a common occurrence that the banshee would howl in groups of three wails,[182] a number classically associated with the Morrígan. This is emphasised further by this trait being originally associated with the badhbh variant of the banshee and spreading to the other named aspects.[183] This makes sense as the crying of crows and ravens was seen as prophetic (see the excerpt from MSS Trinity H.3.17 in Appendix iv) and may be the source of the banshee's cry.

Although not associated directly with water, the banshee is often linked with water. *"She is more commonly imagined to appear close to water, at lakes, rivers or wells."*[184] As has been detailed earlier, the Morrígan is strongly associated with water in a variety of her aspects, water being seen as highly magical in the Celtic worldview.

---

[179] Although other instances of lamenting faery women do occur, as in *Táin Bó Fraích* where Fraech is lamented by one hundred and fifty faery women after his death due to the love the faery kings bore him.
[180] *Foclóir Gaedhilge agus Béarla* – Rev. P.S. Dineen, Dublin, 1927.
[181] *The Banshee: The Irish Death Messenger,* p95.
[182] *Ibid,* p77.
[183] *Ibid,* p77.
[184] *Ibid,* p129.

In this context of being close to water, the banshee takes on one of the traditional roles of the Morrígan, the Washer at the water who foretells death. This is first recorded in folklore by Matthew Archdeacon in 1839, who noted *"Sometimes she (the banshee) be's seen at the sthrame beetlin' the windin' sheet."*[185]

Another more recent indication of her derivation from the Morrígan is found in the 19th century, which is the stupid and even fatal nature of insulting her. Hence we find:

"Better for you to shoot your own mother than fire at the Banshee ... Let her alone while she lets you alone, for an hour's luck never shone on anyone that ever molested the banshee."[186]

An infrequent occurrence associated with the banshee also hints at her derivation from the Morrígan. This occurrence is the calling of more than one banshee for the death of a person. McAnally records *"The honour of being warned by more than one Banshee is, however, very great and comes only to the purest of the pure."*[187]

Briggs also records this belief, recording *"When several keen together it foretells the death of someone very great or holy."*[188] This appears to be a remnant of the concept of Badb (a name for the banshee) being not a single entity, but rather a class of being.

Banshees were often associated with particular noble families. This may be a remnant of the idea of the Goddess as the Bestower of Sovereignty, as the banshee does not tend to bemoan the forthcoming deaths of people of non-noble blood.

The most common colour recorded for the banshee to be seen wearing is white, though in some instances red has also been seen. These colours are also the colours associated with the otherworld and fairy folk in Celtic mythology.

---

[185] *Legends of Connaught* – Matthew Archdeacon, Dublin, 1839, p176.
[186] *Legends and Tales of the Queen's County Peasantry* – J. Keegan, Dublin, p366-74.
[187] *Irish Wonders* – D. R. McAnally, London, 1888, p114.
[188] *Dictionary of Fairies* – Katharine Briggs, London, 1976, p14.

The Bean Nighe – Scottish Faery Washer at the Ford

The Bean Nighe ("Washing Woman") was seen as a member of the faery court, who could be found at the side of desolate streams and pools. Like the Washer at the Ford she washes the bloodstained clothing of those who are about to die. She is also referred to as the ban nighechain ("little washerwoman"); and nigheag na h-ath ("little washer at the ford").

In appearance she is described as small in stature, always dressed in green and has red webbed feet. She is said to have only one nostril, a large protruding front tooth and long pendulous breasts. Grabbing and sucking her breast and claiming to be her foster-child will win the brave person a wish.

Although the Bean Nighe was often seen as an evil portent she was not always an omen of ones own death as in Ireland, and if approached in the correct way she would grant three wishes in classic faery fashion. All you had to do was get between her and the water.

Some versions of the tale say that you must see her first, or she may inflict bodily injury on you, and that she should be caught with the left hand, recalling the association of this side of the body with sorcery in Celtic myth.[189]

If you do this successfully, you can then ask for three wishes and answer three questions. The three questions must be answered truthfully in return for the wishes to be granted, in the manner of the classic traditional exchange between humans and supernatural creatures. Any attempt at deceit immediately forfeits the wishes.

The Bean Nighe was said to be the ghost of women who had died in childbirth, and had to perform their role until the natural time destined for their death came.

---

[189] *A' bhean nighe*, Folklore 9:91-2, 1898.

The Caointeach – The Scottish Weeper

The *Caointeach* or *Caoineag* ("Weeper") is a more ferocious version of the Bean Nighe that does not grant wishes. Anyone interrupting her runs the risk of losing the use of their limbs, as she will strike at them with her wet linen, which removes the function of any limb it strikes.[190]

She is a member of the Fuath class of faery, who are dangerous and malicious spirits associated with water. The Caointeach is rarely seen, and will often be heard wailing in the darkness at waterfalls before a disaster or death affects a clan. Carmichael records in *Carmina Gadelica* that the MacDonald Caointeach was heard to wail for several nights before the Massacre of Glencoe was inflicted on that clan.[191] This led to a song recalling this treachery:

"Little caoineag of the sorrow
Is pouring the tears of her eyes,
Weeping and wailing the fate of Clan MacDonald,
Alas my grief! That ye did not heed her cries."[192]

---

[190] *A Dictionary of Fairies* – Katharine Briggs, 1976, p20.
[191] *Carmina Gadelica*, Vol 2:227.
[192] *Highland Mythology* – E.C. Watson in *Folklore* 5:51, 1908.

The Cyhyraeth – The Welsh Weeper

Like her Scottish counterpart, the *Cyhyraeth* ("Weeper") is rarely seen, but is heard groaning before deaths, especially multiple deaths caused by a disaster or disease.

The noise is reputedly heard in three stages:

"The voice resembles the groaning of sick persons who are to die; heard at first at a distance, then comes nearer, and the last near at hand; so that it is a threefold warning of death. It begins strong, and louder than a sick man can make; the second cry is lower, but not less doleful, but rather more so; the third yet lower, and soft, like the groaning of a sick man almost spent and dying."[193]

She would also wail for natives who died away from home. On the Glamorganshire coast she was said to pass along the sea before a wreck occurred, accompanied by a corpse-light, guiding the drowned souls to the nearest churchyard.

[193] *British Goblins* – Wirt Sikes, 1880, p219-22.

The Gwrach-y-Rhybin – Welsh Banshee

Also in Wales we encounter the *Gwrach-y-Rhybin* ("hag of the mist") - a hideous faery hag who haunts Welsh families, and is also associated with specific places. She has a scary appearance, being winged, with matted black hair, overlong arms, black teeth and a hooked nose.

In the manner of the Banshee, she haunts the old Welsh families, warning of death. Her favourite method was to flap her wings against the window at night and howl the name of the person who would die.[194]

It was rare for anyone to see her as she preferred to stay in the mist, but if seen by a person when they were walking she would cry out as if she was lamenting the person who was going to die. For instance if a man was about to die she would cry *"Oh my husband! My husband!"*[195]

The Gwrach-y-Rhybin was also said to haunt Pennard Castle and the banks of the river Dribble. She echoes the Washer at the Ford in that she was known to bat (splash) the water with her hands when she was seen near a river.

She also has another form, known as the *yr Hen Chrwchwd* ("old hump-backed one"), in which she appears as a shrieking old woman, her cries foretelling the death of a local person.[196]

---

[194] *British Goblins: Welsh Folklore, Fairy Mythology, Legends and Traditions* – Wirt Sikes, 1880, p216-7.
[195] *Ibid.*
[196] *Folklore of Wales* – Anne Ross, Stroud, 2001, p100.

The Laundresses of Night – Penitent Breton Washer at the Ford

The *Laundresses of Night* ("Les Lavandières de nuit") are the Breton version of the penitent woman condemned to wash clothes at the ford for the duration until her sins were paid for. Such sins included breaking the sanctity of the Sabbath or a holy day,[197] committing suicide or drowning,[198] dying unshriven, unbaptised or unconfirmed, or committing infanticide.[199]

More harshly this fate could also be a punishment for such minor misdemeanours as damaging the clothing of the poor by washing it carelessly, or excessively banging it against rocks in order to save soap.[200]

These Washers are more malicious than other types, and may or may not predict death, but will try and entice passers-by to help them wind sheets, and then break their arms.[201] The only way to save yourself if they did persuade you to help them wind sheets was to wind the sheet in the same way as them, as they got bored and let you go. If you wound in the opposite direction as they tried to encourage you, there was no escape and your arms got broken.

---

[197] Souvestre, 1845, p69-75.
[198] *Le Folk-Lore de France (vol 2)* – Paul Sébillot, Oriental and American Library, Paris, 1905, p355.
[199] *Ibid,* p425.
[200] *Traditions et Superstitions de la Basse-Bretagne, Revue Celtique* 1:225-242, 414-435 – R.F. LeMen, 1870.
[201] *Ibid,* p421.

The Washer – Penitent Scottish Washer at the Ford

A variant of the faery Washer at the Ford we will mention briefly is the Washer. Found in the folklore of the island of Skye, a Washer was a woman who died in childbirth having left the laundry unwashed.[202] The Washer had to spend what would have been her normal lifespan had she lived washing at a ford or lake before her soul could move on.

---

[202] *Superstitions of the Highlands & Islands of Scotland* – J.G. Campbell, London, 1900, p43.

13. The Prophetess

The use of prophecy and prediction of the future is one of the most commonly used powers of the Morrígan. In doing so she is indicating that she is a Goddess of Fate, influencing future events.

On some occasions the Morrígan delivers a prophecy to ensure that future events will occur. An example of this is when she prophesied to the bull Donn Cúlainge (the "Brown Bull of Cooley"), warning him that he was to be kidnapped in a cattle raid.

"The Morrígan daughter of Ernmas came from the síd and sat on the pillar-stone in Temair Cúlainge, warning the Donn Cúlainge about the men of Ireland." [203]

After having predicted Cormac's death as the Washer at the Ford, Badb turns up again at the hostel to deliver the prophecy again, doubly emphasising his fate.

"She put her shoulder against the doorpost and began uttering evil prophecies and words of ill omen to the host, so that she said this: "There will be grief in the hostel; there will be mangled bodies in blood; necks will be without heads above the floor of Da Choca's hostel." After that the Badb went from them." [204]

Her best-known prophecy is undoubtedly the victory prophecy given after the Túatha Dé Danann have defeated the Fomorians. This is a double prophecy, of two parts. The first part is positive, and can be seen as a short-term prophecy of celebration in success. The second part though is an apocalyptic prediction of doom, of the kind found in many other religions for the end of the world.

This prophecy embodies the nature of the Morrígan extremely well. It combines the two opposing principles of order and chaos. The first part of the prophecy is about a time of bounty, happiness and strength, everything in order. Hence the earth and sky are in their appropriate places, the cup is full of honey, and the woods are full of stags. The military might shown in victory is strongly emphasised by spears, shields and forts.

---

[203] *Táin Bó Cúailnge.*
[204] *Bruiden Da Chocae.*

The second half of the prophecy is the apocalyptic end of the world scenario found in almost all religions (e.g. the Norse Ragnarok and Christian Revelations of St John.)

The breakdown of the social order is forecast, as is the breakdown of the family unit, something very important to the Celts. The lines *"fishless seas, Bad judgements by old men, False precedents of the lawgivers"*[205] seem disturbingly appropriate today.

However when we consider the second prophecy we should consider that the destruction and return of chaos described by it represents a universal phenomena. This is the cyclic nature of existence – civilizations rise and fall, to be replaced by new civilizations. The ruling order changes, even if the structure seems to repeat a pattern.

---

[205] *Cath Maige Tuired.*

The Prophecy

"Peace to the sky, sky to the earth,
earth beneath sky, strength in each;
a cup very full, full of honey,
honour enough, summer in winter;
spear supported by shield,
shields supported by forts,
forts fierce eager for battle,
fleece from sheep, woods full of stags,
forever destructions have departed,
mast on trees, a branch drooping-down,
drooping from growth
wealth for a son, a son very learned
neck of bull in yoke, a bull from a song
knots in woods, wood for a fire
fire as wanted
palisades new and bright
salmon their victory, the Boyne their hostel
hostel with an excellence of size
new growth after spring
in autumn horses increase
the land held secure
land recounted with excellence of word
Be might to the eternal much excellent woods
peace to sky be this nine times eternal."

"I shall not see a world that will be dear to me.
Summer without flowers, cows without milk,
Women without modesty, men not brave,
Conquests without a king.
Woods without mast, fishless seas,
Bad judgements by old men,
False precedents of the lawgivers.
Every man a betrayer, each son a robber,
The son will enter his father's bed
The father also in the bed of the son,
A brother becomes his own brother-in-law!
None will look for a woman outside his own house.
O evil time, deception, deception."[206]

---

[206] *Cath Maige Tuired.*

124

Fedelm

In *Táin Bó Cúailnge* a prophetess is described who is clearly another guise of the Morrígan. As Queen Medb is about to leave Cruachain with her army she sees a beautiful maiden in a chariot drawn by two black horses approaching. She has yellow hair in three plaits, two up and one hanging down to her calves (recalling the faery associations of the banshee, and also being the triple motif). A woman alone in a chariot in the myths usually indicates a guise of the Morrígan, as it is the action of a warrior.

In her hands she has a weaver's beam of white bronze,[207] and when asked who she is, she replies, *"I am Fedelm the poetess of Connaught"*.[208] Medb asks if she has the power of prophecy called *imbass forosna* ("divination which illuminates"),[209] and Fedelm answers affirmatively.

Imbass forosna can be interpreted in two ways. The first is a three-day process that involved a specific diet and sleeping patterns. However the stories indicate a more immediate process, suggesting the second method. This is the chewing of the flesh of the thumb to gain insight and wisdom.[210]

She then tells Queen Medb that Cú Chulainn will perform heroic deeds and decimate her army. When Medb asks why she has come bearing bad news, Fedelm replies that she is promoting Medb's interests by gathering together the warriors of the great provinces to

---

[207] In some versions of the tale she is actually weaving a fringe, e.g. *The Book of Leinster*. The weaving motif is also highly significant, as it is classically associated with the weaving of fate, e.g. the Norns in Norse myth and Fates in Greek myth.
[208] In *The Book of Leinster* version Fedelm says *"I am Fedelm the prophetess from Síd Chrúachna"* making her faery connection evident.
[209] *Imbas Forosnai* – N.K. Chadwick, in *Scottish Gaelic Studies IV* 2:97-135, 1935.
[210] E.g. when Demne sticks his thumb in his mouth after being burned by the salmon of wisdom, and when Gwion Bach sticks his thumb in his mouth after being burned by the three drops of Awen from the cauldron of Cerridwen. In both cases the individual is transformed, Demne becomes Fionn MacCumhill, and Gwion Bach becomes Taliesin.

go with her to fight (for although Cú Chulainn will be heroic he does get killed).

Fedelm is also mentioned in the conversation between Cú Chulainn and the maiden Emer. They are talking in riddles using magical place and people names to confuse Emer's maidens, who are listening in. Her name occurs between other names which all refer to guises of the Morrígan, implying that she is one of these as well:

"The foam of the two steeds of Emain Macha; over the Morrigu's Garden ... over the Marrow of the Woman Fedelm ... over the Washing-place of the horses of Dea."[211]

Emer also refers to her when setting the tasks Cú Chulainn must perform to win her hand in marriage, *"Where the quick froth of Fedelm makes Brea leap."*[212]

---

[211] *Tochmarc Émire.*
[212] *Tochmarc Émire.*

Scáthach's Prophecy

When Cú Chulainn leaves Scáthach's island she gives him the prophecy of his future that she has promised him after his arrival. This is described in the text known as *Verba Scáthaige*[213] and foretells much of what will occur during the *Táin*.

"Then Scáthach foretold to him what was in store for him and told him of his end through Vision which illumines:[214]

When thou art a peerless champion, great extremity awaits thee, alone against the vast herd. Warriors will be set aside against thee, necks will be broken by thee, thy sword will strike strokes to the rear against Sétante's[215] *gory stream. Hard-bladed, he will cut the trees by the sign of slaughters, by manly feats. Cows will be carried off from thy hill, captives will be forfeited by thy people; harried by the troop for a fortnight, thy cattle will walk the passes. Thou wilt be alone in great hardship against the host. Scarlet gushes of blood will strike upon many variously-cloven shields. A band of parasites that thou wilt adhere to will bring away many people and oxen. Many wounds will be inflicted upon thee, Cú Chulainn. You will suffer a wound of revenge in one of the encounters at the final breach. From your red-pronged weapon there will be defeat, men pierced against the furious wave, against the whale equipped for exploits, a whale performing feats with blows. Women will wail and beat hands in their troop, Medb and Ailill boast of it. A sick-bed awaits thee in face of slaughters of great ferocity. I see the very glossy Finnbennach216 in great rage against Donn Cúailnge."*[217]

---

[213] The text was originally probably part of a lost 8th century MSS called *Cín Dromna Snechta*, subsequently reproduced in later MSS which have survived.

[214] This is a translation of *imbass forossndi* – "the power which illuminates", also ascribed to the prophetess Fedelm, and further linking both characters as guises of the Goddess.

[215] Setante is Cú Chulainn's birth name before he gains his more familiar warrior name.

[216] The White-horned Bull, as Donn Cuailgne is the Brown Bull.

[217] Five versions of this MSS (*Verba Scáthaige*) exist, the earliest of which is the 14th century *MSS Rawlinson B512* in the Bodlean Library.

14. Morgan Le Fay and the Arthurian Myths

A number of writers have suggested a link between the Morrígan and the sorceress Morgan Le Fay in the Arthurian cycle of myths. But apart from the similarity of names are there other strands of commonality to justify this association? And if we are going to look at Morgan then we also have to look at the Lady of the Lake, Nimue or Vivian .

The best known versions of the Arthurian tale are the polished version presented by Sir Thomas Malory, *Le Morte D'Arthur* (1485), and the earlier recension of Geoffrey of Monmouth, *Vita Merlini* (1150). However, as with the Irish tales, which were drawn from a number of different sources and presented in different versions, so these later and best-known versions of the Arthurian saga draw on a diverse collection of earlier strands from different areas.

Morgan Le Fay first appears in *Vita Merlini* in 1150. Her name itself links her to the Morrígan in several ways. As has already been discussed, Morrígan can mean "Sea Queen", and the name Morgan translates as "born of the sea", from *"Mor"* meaning *"sea"* and *"gan"* meaning *"birth"*. "Le Fay" is a reference to the faery as the meaning of the words, indicating her otherworldly nature.

In *Vita Merlini*, Morgan is the chief of nine sisters,[218] but there is no suggestion of any relationship between Morgan and King Arthur; she is simply his healer:

"That is the place where nine sisters exercise a kindly rule over those who come to them from our land. The one who is first among them has greater skill in healing, as her beauty surpasses that of her sisters. Her name is Morgen, and she has learned the uses of all plants in curing the ills of the body. She knows, too, the art of changing her shape, of flying through the air, like Daedalus, on strange wings. At will, she is now at Brest, now at Chartres, now at Pavia; and at will she glides down from the sky on to your shores. They say she had taught astrology to her sisters - Moronoe, Mazoe,

---

[218] This has survived into modern day practice, with the Nine Morgens being celebrated by Goddess groups including the Goddess Temple in Glastonbury.

Gliten, Glitonea, Gliton, Tyronoe, and Thiten, - Thiten, famous for her lyre."[219]

This gathering of nine sisters on the isle of Avalon is extremely similar to the much earlier Roman account of the island of Sena (Sein) off the coast of Brittany given by Pomponius Mela.[220] He recorded there being nine virgin priestesses on the island, *"The Gauls call them Senae, and they believe them to be endowed with extraordinary gifts, to rouse the seas and the wind by their incantations, to turn themselves into whatsoever animal form they may choose, to cure diseases which among others are incurable, to know what is to come and to foretell it."*

In Chrétien de Troyes' *Erec and Enide* (1160), Morgan Le Fay is a giver of healing ointments, and friend of Guingamar, the Lord of Avalon, and is one of the guests at the wedding of Erec and Enide.

Morgan is first described as being King Arthur's sister in *"Draco Normannicus"* by Etienne de Rouen in 1169.

The first mention of Morgan in *Le Morte D'Arthur* (Book 1, chapter 3) tells us that: *"the third sister Morgan le Fay was put to school in a nunnery, and there she learned so much that she was a great clerk of necromancy."* That Morgan should learn the practice of necromancy in a convent with the nuns is rather bizarre, but does emphasise her magical ability.

In *Le Morte D'Arthur*, Morgan is married to the Welsh King Uriens, who is described in *The Mabinogion* as the partner of Modron, a Welsh Goddess, who is also linked to the Morrígan. Strictly speaking Morgan (or Morcant) is a man's name. The feminine version of the name is Morgain (or Morgue or Morgne).

It is interesting to note that there was a sixth-century Cumbrian ruler called Urien Rheged, who presided over a loose coalition of kings. Urien had a loose ally called Morcant Bulc - a man who subsequently plotted to assassinate him. Looking at the names of the main protagonists, it seems likely that this might have been Malory's inspiration for the plot-line in *Le Morte D'Arthur* where Morgan Le Fay attempts to kill both Arthur and Uriens (her husband).

---

[219] *Vita Merlini.*
[220] *De Situ Orbis* – Mela, Book 3, chapter 6.

The bestowal of the sword Excalibur on Arthur by the Lady of the Lake is clearly a bestowal of sovereignty onto the rightful candidate. This motif combined with the faery connection indicates the Morrígan connection:

"And in the midst of the lake Arthur was ware of an arm clothed in white samite, that held a fair sword in that hand ... With that they saw a damsel going upon the lake. What damsel is that? said Arthur. That is the Lady of the Lake, said Merlin; and within that lake is a rock, and therein is as fair a place as any on earth,[221] and richly beseen; and this damsel will come to you anon, and then speak ye fair to her that she will give you that sword ... Damsel, said Arthur, what sword is that, that yonder the arm holdeth above the water? I would it were mine, for I have no sword. Sir Arthur, king, said the damsel, that sword is mine, and if ye will give me a gift when I ask it you, ye shall have it. By my faith, said Arthur, I will give you what gift ye will ask. Well! said the damsel, go ye into yonder barge, and row yourself to the sword, and take it and the scabbard with you, and I will ask my gift when I see my time."[222]

Nimue as the Lady of the Lake twice saves Arthur from Morgan's magic and devious plans, showing how the Bestower of Sovereignty protects the rightful king as long as he keeps faith and is worthy. It is also reminiscent of the love-hate relationship of the Morrígan with Cú Chulainn, where she alternately helps and hinders him.

Following the war with the five kings, King Arthur, King Uriens, and Sir Accolon go on a hunt.[223] With their horses exhausted, the heroes find themselves by a great lake where they see a silk-clad ship approach. Having gone on board, they are greeted by twelve damsels, feasted and shown to separate chambers.

As they lay in a drug-induced sleep, each is magically transported away by Morgan. Uriens is returned to Camelot, Arthur is sent to the prison of the evil Sir Damas (minus Excalibur and scabbard), and Sir Accolon to a well near the manor of the good Sir Ontzlake, younger brother of Sir Damas.

---

[221] This is clearly a description of an entrance to the faery world, which is usually in a mound or a body of water.
[222] *Le Morte D'Arthur*, chapter 25.
[223] *Ibid*, Book 4.

Morgan then sends her lover, Sir Accolon, to fight Arthur, having previously extracted a promise from him to fight an unspecified knight at her pleasure. Having copied Excalibur and its magical scabbard, Morgan arms Sir Accolon with them. Morgan sends a damsel to Arthur with a fake Excalibur and scabbard.

Sir Accolon is prevailing when Nimue intervenes and strengthens Arthur's blow so he is able to disarm his opponent and grab the real Excalibur. Accolon then surrenders and confesses, but dies of his wounds soon after anyway.

Morgan subsequently tries to steal Excalibur and the scabbard again, and goes to the nunnery where Arthur is recovering from his wounds. She only manages to take the scabbard because he sleeps with the sword in his hand.[224]

When Arthur wakes he sets off in pursuit of Morgan, but she casts the scabbard into a deep lake, essentially putting it out of human reach by moving it into the magical otherworldly realm of water (recalling the practice of throwing votive offerings into bodies of water). Morgan then uses her shape-changing powers to disguise herself and her entourage as standing stones to escape further pursuit, again showing her magical abilities.

Later Morgan sends a damsel to give Arthur a rich mantle embellished with precious stones, in atonement for her past transgressions. However she has laced the mantle with poison. Nimue intervenes, saving Arthur, who makes the damsel put it on; she then dies, burnt to coals.

When Arthur is mortally wounded Morgan is one of the "three Queens" from the Isle of Avalon who take him away to be healed. The others are the Queen of Northgalis (North Wales) and the Queen of the Wastelands. As Morgan was married to the Welsh King Uriens it is possible these other two queens are representations of her, showing the triple motif often associated with the Morrígan.

Another representation of the Morrígan we find in the Arthurian mythos is the character of Anna. This name is clearly derived from Anu or Áine, both forms of the Morrígan in Irish myth. She is first

---

[224] Here she tries to remove his sovereignty, but only succeeds in removing the protection offered by the scabbard.

mentioned by Geoffrey of Monmouth in 1136, as sister of King Arthur, and daughter of Uther Pendragon and Queen Ygerna.[225]

Anna is said to be married to King Lot of Lodonesia (Gododdin), by whom she became the mother of Gwalchmai (Gawain) and Medrod (Mordred). These knights are subsequently attributed as children of the Lady Morgause, and this is where things become confused.

In Le Morte D'Arthur, Morgause was the half-sister of Arthur who married Lot. She was the mother of Gawain, Gaheris, Agravain, Gareth, and Mordred. Mordred is the result of an encounter between Morgause and her half-brother Arthur, who was unaware of their relationship.

Modern writers have often attributed Mordred's parentage to an incestuous union between Morgan Le Fay and Arthur, but this is not something that is found in the tales. Morgan and Morgause have sometimes been merged into one character by modern writers, but this is symptomatic of the way the stories have continued to change even in recent centuries.

In the late 14th century poem Sir Gawain and the Green Knight, Morgan sends the Green Knight to court to test the courage of the knights, seeing who will fight him. Here she is being shown in the role of War Goddess again, testing heroes.

This tale is clearly derived from the Irish tale of the Feast of Bricriu. In this tale Cú Chulainn is arguing with two other heroes about which of them is worthy of the title hero. They go to a giant who offers to let them cut his head off in return for him returning the favour the next day. Only Cú Chulainn is brave enough to accept, and the giant does not behead him but declares him worthy.

In Sir Gawain and the Green Knight, the Green Knight arrives clad all in green, bearing a huge green steel axe and a holly branch, showing both his faery association and his role as a champion of the Earth Goddess.

The Green Knight challenges the knights of Arthur's court to the "Beheading Game". He will allow a knight to behead him, but then the knight must do the same a year and a day later. Arthur is shamed by

---

[225] History of the Kings of Britain – Geoffrey of Monmouth, 1136.

his knight's lack of courage and steps forward, but Gawain persuades Arthur to let him stand in.

Gawain beheads the knight with his axe. All the court is amazed after the beheading when the Green Knight picks up his head and leaves. As he departs he reminds Gawain of his vow and to come and seek him out when the time is up.

Whilst on his quest to find the Green Knight, Gawain is helped by a mysterious lady in the castle he is staying at. She offers him a magical ring of red gold with a jewel in, which he refuses. She then offers a green and gold silk girdle that protects the bearer from all magical attack and prevents him from being overcome, which he accepts.

Gawain allows the Green Knight to strike him, but although he makes a mighty blow it only makes a faint cut on his neck. The Green Knight realises that Gawain possesses the girdle and chastises him for his lack of courage. Gawain then asks the Green Knight his name, and is told:

"Bernlak de Hautdesert am I called in this land. Morgain le Fay dwelleth in mine house, and through knowledge of clerkly craft hath she taken many. For long time was she the mistress of Merlin, who knew well all you knights of the court. Morgain the Goddess is she called therefore, and there is none so haughty but she can bring him low. She sent me in this guise to yon fair hall to test the truth of the renown that is spread abroad of the valour of the Round Table. She taught me this marvel to betray your wits, to vex Guinevere and fright her to death by the man who spake with his head in his hand at the high table. That is she who is at home, that ancient lady, she is even thine aunt, Arthur's half-sister, the daughter of the Duchess of Tintagel, who afterward married King Uther.[226]

Much of what we now perceive as the Arthurian mythos comes from French origins. To this end we must also examine the French tales for further manifestations of the Morrígan as Morgan Le Fay. This is particularly evident in the anonymous 14th century French poem *Roman d'Ogier le Danois*, and *Ly Myreur des Histors* by Jean d'Outremeuse (1338-1400), both of which recount tales of the hero Ogier the Dane, a figure who mirrors King Arthur as the returning hero.

---

[226] *Sir Gawain and the Green Knight.*

Ogier the Dane is a paladin in the court of King Charlemagne. At his birth six faeries give him gifts, to be the bravest, the handsomest, the strongest, the most successful, and the most susceptible of knights. The final faery was Morgue le Faye (i.e. Morgan Le Fay), who said she would take him at the end of his life to live in love with her on the Isle of Avalon.

When he is one hundred years old Ogier goes on a journey to Avalon, and is shipwrecked on the island shores. A disembodied voice tells him to *"fear nothing, but enter the castle which I will show thee."* [227] He goes to the castle and finds a horse called Papillon,[228] which conducts him to Morgue La Faye.

Morgue La Faye gives Ogier a magical ring that makes him young again and removes all infirmities and illness. She also gives him a crown that makes him forget his past, and introduces him to King Arthur. We can see the sovereignty motif here with the crown and also the ring that transforms age to youth, which is reminiscent of the transformation of hag to maiden.

Two hundred years later when France is invaded by the Paynims, Morgue removes the crown from Ogier's head, restoring his memory, and sends him to defend France and rout the invaders. He does this and then returns to Morgue in Avalon, where he has remained ever since.

---

[227] *Roman d'Ogier le Danois.*
[228] Note the horse motif associated with the Goddess occurring again.

15. Other Manifestations of the Morrígan

As will have become clear throughout this book, the Morrígan assumes a wide range of guises. Although she is primarily considered an Irish goddess, her influence can be seen throughout the British Isles, and also in France.

Throughout the early Irish literature the influence of the Morrígan can be felt in some form in almost every tale. Her presence has never really faded, as she has taken on a variety of guises as various faery figures and local goddesses. Many of these figures are not immediately obvious as guises of the Morrígan, and might even be thought of as dis-guises of the Morrígan.

However, when we look at her roles, names, symbols and myths, it becomes self-evident that she has continued to play a role in the development of folklore, literature and even the naming of places.

To put all the material covered into a clear perspective that covers the whole spectrum of her guises and disguises, this chapter covers all the different goddesses and beings that are associated with the Morrígan, as aspects or derivatives of her.

Áine

Áine is a Faery Queen who occurs in several tales. As with many faery figures, we can consider it possible that she is the survival of an earlier Goddess figure.

Áine means *brightness*, *"heat"* or *"speed"*, and she is mentioned in connection with the Morrígan by some writers. *"And as to Áine, that some said was a daughter of Manannan, but some said was the Morrigu herself."*[229]

Let us consider the areas of commonality between them. Áine had a revengeful nature, which is certainly also true of the Morrígan. In one instance this actually led to a battle being fought,[230] which is highly appropriate. Áine was also known as *Lair Derg* (red mare) showing a connection to the Horse Goddess guise of the Morrígan.

Áine gave gifts of poetry and music, showing her association with words and sounds, which she again has in common with the Morrígan. She was known as Leanan Sídhe ("the Sweetheart of the Sidhe"), demonstrating her links to the faery folk, of whom the Morrígan is the Faery Queen.

By the 17th century Áine is being described in the role of a banshee. As a weeping banshee she brings word of the imminent death of Maurice Fitzgerald in 1642,[231] indicating that by this time she had been assimilated into the faery role of the death-messenger.

In the 19th century Áine is being depicted combing her hair on the banks of the Camóg river and at Lough Gur,[232] showing how she was seen in the common view as a faery being associated with the banshee.

---

[229] *Irish Myths and Legends* – Lady Gregory, 1904, p98.
[230] Magh Mucruimhe.
[231] *Gearóid Iarla agus an Dratíocht* – D. Ó hÓgáin, 1979, p240.
[232] *Popular Tales of Ireland VI: Gearóid Iarla and Áine N'Chliar*, D, Fitzgerald, 1879, 4:185-99.

Andraste

We have already suggested that the British Goddess Andraste, invoked by Boudicca before attacking the Romans, and described as "a savage warrior Goddess" was a guise of the Morrígan. This is discussed earlier in chapter 4 *The Queen of Battle.*

Dio Cassius in his *History of Rome* says that Andraste was the Icenians' name for *"Victory"*, recalling the Greek Goddess Nike, whose name also means Victory, and that she enjoyed their especial reverence. Nike was one of the few Greek Goddesses depicted with wings (along with Artemis and Athena).

It is possible that the name Andraste was a title of the Morrígan, used by Boudicca to incite her troops, as we know that she was associated with vocal encouragement before battle as practiced by the Celts.

Boudicca released a hare for Andraste before going into battle as a form of divination, the direction the hare ran indicating victory. This is why the hare is often given as sacred to Andraste.

The hare connection with Andraste is seen in later folklore as a witch motif in Ireland and Scotland, and also in the tale of *The Venomous Boar of Glen Glass*, where the raven is eating a dead hare when it warns the hero Diarmaid. The hare is also connected to the hag through such folk tales, as discussed previously.

Due to the similarity in their names it has been suggested there is a connection between Andraste and the Gallic Fertility Goddess Andarta. Although there is no supporting evidence for this, it is an interesting suggestion, when considering the Earth Goddess guises of the Morrígan.

Anu/Danu

"The Morrígan ... and it is from her other name "Danu" the Paps of Ana in Luchair are named, as well as the Túatha Dé Danann."[233]

"Badb and Macha and Anu, i.e. the Morrígan, from whom the Paps of Anu in Luachair are named, were the three daughters of Ernmas the witch."[234]

As already mentioned, Danu and the Morrígan are equated, both directly and indirectly, in several references. In *The Book of Lecan*, the two are directly equated, whereas the prophetic dream of Eochaid the Fir Bolg king in *First Battle of Moytura* implies the same equation of the two Goddesses by its symbolism (the great flock of black birds representing the Túatha Dé Danann).

During the boasting before the battle with the Fir Bolgs, Danu is mentioned in the same sentence as the trio of guises commonly referred to as the Morrígna, implying a direct link to the Morrígan.

"We will go with you, said the women, that is, Badb, Macha, Morrígan and Danu."[235]

Danu means "river", and may be the root of the name of the river Danube in Germany, where the Celts were known to live. We have shown earlier that the Morrígan is often linked with rivers. Danu is also recorded in some sources as Danand and Danann (and hence Túatha Dé Danann), and Anu is also recorded in places as Anand and Anann.

Danu was married to the Death God Bilé, with whom she produces the Daghda. As a guise of the Morrígan it is an obvious match, to be wed to a God of Death.

This Earth Goddess and her connection to the Morrígan are considered in more detail within chapter 5 *The Earth Goddess*.

---

[233] *The Book of Lecan.*
[234] *The Book of Leinster.*
[235] *Cath Muighe Tuireadh.*

138

Aoibheall

Aoibheall is another Faery Queen, who also plays the role of the death messenger, in a similar manner to the banshee or Washer at the Ford.
Before the battle of Clontarf (1014) Aoibheall forewarns the king of his death, and also predicts victory for the Irish.

By calling her appearance that of a Faery Queen, and describing her under one of her many guises, the Morrígan could still be honoured by those who knew without offending their Christian community.

The prediction of victory is a classic function of the Morrígan. That a manifestation of the Goddess as a crow over the battle also occurred indicating an Irish victory adds to this connection.

After the battle Aoibheall also bestows sovereignty on one of King Brian's sons, demonstrating further qualities of the Morrígan as the Bestower of Sovereignty (see chapter 7 *The Bestower of Sovereignty*).

Banshee

The Banshee is a female faery figure who forewarns of death, usually to noble families. This figure from Irish folklore shows a number of characteristics in common with the Morrígan and is clearly derived from her.

Across Ireland there are three main names associated with the banshee, bean sí, bean chaointe and badhbh. Bean sí translates literally as *faery woman*, bean chaointe as *keening woman*, and badhbh as *scald crow*. All of these names are obviously linked with the Morrígan, in her role as Faery Queen, her role as the Washer at the Ford, and in her guise of Badhbh.

Banshees are usually described as being hideously ugly old hags or beautiful women with long golden hair and white dresses. This is a classic faery description recalling the Morrígan as Faery Queen.

It is recorded as a common occurrence that the banshee would howl in groups of three wails,[236] a number classically associated with the Morrígan. Although not associated directly with water, the banshee is often linked with water. *"She is more commonly imagined to appear close to water, at lakes, rivers or wells."*[237]

Banshees were often associated with particular noble families. This may be a remnant of the idea of the Goddess as the Bestower of Sovereignty, as the banshee does not bemoan the forthcoming deaths of people of non-noble blood.

The most common colour banshee is seen wearing is white, though in some instances red has also been seen. These colours are also the colours associated with the otherworld and fairy folk in Celtic mythology.

A full discussion of the development of the Banshee from the Morrígan in Irish folklore is given in chapter 10 *The Washer at the Ford*.

---

[236] *The Banshee: The Irish Death Messenger* – Patricia Lysaght, p77.
[237] *Ibid*, p129.

Bean Nighe

The Bean Nighe is a Scottish version of the faery Washer at the Ford, who foretells death, and could be found at the side of desolate streams and pools. She was seen as a member of the faery court, who like the Washer at the Ford she washes the bloodstained clothing of those who are about to die. She is also called the ban nighechain ("little washerwoman"); and nigheag na h-ath ("little washer at the ford").

She was small in stature, always dressed in green and had red webbed feet. She was said to have only one nostril, a large protruding front tooth and long pendulous breasts. Grabbing and sucking her breast and claiming to be her foster-child would win the brave person a wish.

Although the Bean Nighe was often seen as an evil portent, she was not always an omen of ones own death as in Ireland, and if approached in the correct way she would grant three wishes in classic faery fashion. All you had to do was get between her and the water.

Some versions of the tale say that you must see her first, or she may inflict bodily injury on you, and that she should be caught with the left hand, recalling the association of this side of the body with sorcery in Celtic myth.[238]

You could then ask for three wishes in return for answering three questions. The three questions had to be answered truthfully in return for the wishes to be granted, in the manner of the classic traditional exchange between humans and supernatural creatures. Any attempt at deceit immediately forfeited the wishes.

The Bean Nighe was said to be the ghost of women who had died in childbirth, and had to perform their role until the natural time destined for their death came.

A fuller discussion of this Scottish manifestation of the Washer at the Ford is presented in chapter 10 *The Washer at the Ford.*

---

[238] *A' bhean nighe*, Folklore 9, 1898, p91-2.

Bé Néit

"She is the Badb of battle and is called Bé Néit "'the wife of Néit'."[239]

"Néit, i.e. the God of Battle. Nemain is his wife"; "Bé Néit ... Nemon was his wife. This couple was venomous indeed."[240]

The name Bé Néit seems to function more as a title than be the name of a goddess, and is discussed throughout the book. The name functions as a link, equating several of the many guises of the Morrígan in Irish myth. As Néit was described as the God of Battle, it emphasises her role as a Battle Goddess.

One later reference puts her in the role of the Bestower of Victory in battle, referring to the druids' divinatory attempts to predict victory:

"Until they might learn upon which of the bands the fortune of the battle would descend and remain, and upon which of them battle-mourning Bé Néit would establish her mighty power."[241]

---

[239] *Tochmarc Emire*, 10th century.
[240] *Cormac's Glossary.*
[241] *The Banquet of Dun na n-Gedh and the Battle of Magh Rath* – John O'Donovan, 1842.

Black Annis

Black Annis is an English figure who seems to be a survival of a guise of the Morrígan as the hag of winter. Black Annis was also known as Black Agnes or Cat Anna (it has been suggested that this name could be a corruption of the name Cailleach). She was a blue-faced hag who lived in a cave in the Dane Hills, in Leicestershire.

The name Annis may be derived from the Goddess as Anu or Danu. The name "Dane Hills" may also have been derived from Danu as well, although it has been suggested that this place name could also derive from Dannet, the surname of the owner of the hills.

Black Annis lived in a cave, called "Black Annis' Bower Close". She dug the cave out of the rock with her own long nails, which some tales say were made of iron. The cave had a great oak in front of it, behind which she hid to leap out to catch and devour stray children and lambs.

The iron claws are significant as they show that Annis is more likely to be derived from a Goddess and not from the faery, who are well known for their dislike of iron.

One version of the tale has Black Annis turning to stone if she comes out in daylight, recalling the Cailleach Bheur turning into stone for the summer.

Black Annis was seen as a very real threat and affected the Leicestershire area greatly. The common people did not have window-glass in those days, so anti-witch-herbs were tied above the apertures to stop Black Annis reaching inside with her very long arms and grabbing their babies.

Some writers have suggested that this is the reason why Leicester cottages only had one small window. In reality houses used to be taxed per window, so one window in a house was a common occurrence, but this is a far less romantic reason.

Every year on Easter Monday (known as Black Monday in this instance in honour of Black Annis), it was a local custom to hold a mock-hare hunt from her cave to the Mayor of Leicester's house. The bait was actually a dead cat rather than a hare, and it was drenched in aniseed.

The cat was probably used to symbolise her under her name of Cat Anna. The use of aniseed, a herb that was thought to protect from magic, also shows that this ceremony was done as a protective ritual.

Towards the end of the eighteenth century the hunt gave way to an annual event known as the Dane Hills Fair. Despite this, a description from 1941 shows that her memory was still alive and well in the twentieth century:

"Black Annis lived in the Danehills. She was ever so tall and had a blue face and had long white teeth and she ate people. She only went out when it was dark ... when she ground her teeth people could hear her in time to bolt their doors and keep well away from the window ... When Black Annis howled you could hear her five miles away and then even the poor folk in the huts fastened skins across the window and put witch-herbs above it to keep her away safe."[242]

We may observe here that being able to hear her voice from miles away when Annis howled recalls the howls and shrieks of the Morrígan before battles in the Irish myths.

Black Annis also demonstrated the ability to prophesy death like the Morrígan. She prophesied that King Richard III would die when he went past her on his way to the battle at Bosworth and his spurs struck a stone pillar on the bridge.

Annis was said to have made a comment along the lines of, *"It will be his head that will hit that stone when he comes back"*. After losing the battle, the crown and his life, his naked body was thrown across the saddle of a horse and with his head hanging down as low as the stirrups, it hit that very same stone that his spurs had struck.[243]

The poet, John Heyrick Jnr, wrote of her in the 18th century:-

"Where down the plain the winding pathway falls,
From Glen-field, to Lester's ancient walls;
Nature, or art, with imitative power,
Far in the Glenn has plac'd Black Annis's Bower.

---

[242] *Forgotten Folk Tales of the English Counties* – R.L. Tongue, 1970.
[243] *Leicestershire and Rutland* – Arthur Mee, 1937.

An oak, the pride of all the mossy dell,
Spreads its broad arms above the stony cell;
And many a bush, with hostile thorns arrayed,
Forbids the secret cavern to invade;
Whilst delving vales each way meander round,
And violet banks with redolence abound.

Here, if the uncouth song of former days
Soil not the page with Falsehood's artful lays,
Black Annis held her solitary reign,
The dread and wonder of the neighbouring plain.
The shephered grieved to view his waning flock,
And traced his firstlings to the gloomy rock.
No vagrant children culled the flow'rets then,
For infant blood oft stained the gory den.

Not Sparta's mount,[244] for infant tears renown'd,
Echo'd more frequently the piteous sound.
Oft the gaunt Maid the frantic Mother curs'd,
Whom Britain's wolf with savage nipple nurs'd;
Whom Lester's sons beheld, aghast the scene,
Nor dared to meet the Monster of the Green.

'Tis said the soul of mortal man recoil'd
To view Black Annis's eye, so fierce and wild;
Vast talons, foul with human flesh, there grew
In place of hands, and her features livid blue,
Glar'd in her visage; whilst her obscene waist
Warm skins of human victims embrac'd.

But Time, than Man more certain, tho' more slow,
At length 'gainst Annis drew his sable bow;
The great decree the pious shepherds bless'd,
And general joy the general fear confess'd.

Not without terror they the cave survey,
Where hung the monstrous trophies of her sway:
'Tis said, that in the rock large rooms were found,
Scoop'd with her claws beneath the flinty ground;
In these the swains her hated body threw,
But left the entrance still to future view,

---

[244] A reference to Mount Taygetus, where children were exposed to the elements to see if they lived or died in ancient Spartan society.

That children's children might the tale rehearse,
And bards record it in their tuneful verse.

But in these listless days, the idle bard
Gives to the wind all themes of cold regard;
Forgive, then, if in rough, unpolished song,
An unskilled swain the dying tale prolong.

And you, ye Fair, whom Nature's scenes delight,
If Annis' Bower your vagrant steps invite,
Ere the bright sun Aurora's car succeed,
Or dewy evening quench the thirsty mead,
Forbear with chilling censures to refuse
Some gen'rous tribute to the rustic muse.
A violet or common daisy throw,
Such gifts such as Maro's lovely nymphs bestow;
Then shall your Bard survive the critic's frown,
And in your smiles enjoy his best renown."[245]

Black Annis is also described as dwelling on the moors and hillsides of the Scottish Highlands. There she is described as a witch-like hideous old hag with blue skin and a single piercing eye. If she captures human beings, she eats them, and is often referred to as sitting on a pile of bones outside her cave, with an oak tree (as with the English version).

She would carry humans off into her cave, suck them dry of blood[246] and eat their flesh before draping their flayed skins out to dry on the oak's branches. She then made the skins into a skirt to wear. As she was also said to prey on animals, local shepherds would blame any lost sheep on her hunger.

Another form of Black Annis in Scotland was a weather spirit said to watch over the gales on the Firth of Cromarty. This area is known for its spasmodic squalls that can blow up in moments. As a result she had a reputation for treachery, turning up when least expected. She was often called Gentle Annie or Annis, probably in propition to try and calm her temper.

---

[245] *County Folklore Printed Extracts No. 3, Leicestershire & Rutland –* C.J. Billson, 1895, p4-6.
[246] As with the Baobhan Sith, Lamia and Mis the blood-sucking theme is apparent.

Boand & Bovinda

Boand is an Irish river and cattle Goddess. The name Boand (or Boann or Boind) means *"White Cow"*. One of her titles is *Agda* which means *Cow Goddess.*[247]

There are a number of parallels between Boand and the Morrígan that suggest this may be another guise of the same great Goddess. The repetition motif is one that is sometimes used to imply different aspects of the same deity.

Hence the Daghda's sexual union with Indech's daughter, who is sometimes called Boand, after he has already joined with the Morrígan at the ford may be implying that the two Goddesses are in fact one and the same.

In another tale the Daghda desires Boann, and sends her husband Elcmar on an errand. He makes love with Boann, but he also stops the sun, so that nine months pass for them and she is able to give birth to Angus Og, whilst for Elcmar only one day passes and he is thus tricked into not knowing what has occurred.

Boand is referred to by the title *rígan*, (the Irish word for Queen), the same term used to describe the Morrígan. In the *Dindshenchas* the gushing waters of Nechtain's well injures her in a manner which exactly parallels the wounds the Morrígan receives from Cú Chulainn when she attacks him in animal forms at the ford. Hence:

"As thrice she walked round about the well heedlessly,
Three waves burst from it; whence came the death of Boand.
They came each wave of them against a limb; they disfigure the soft-blooming woman, A wave against her foot, a wave against her perfect eye; the third wave shatters one hand."

The river Boyne is named after the Goddess Boand, and was said to be her dwelling place. The Gallic cow Goddess Bovinda, whose name means *White Cow*, can be seen as being another manifestation of Boand, and hence the Morrígan. Titles for her reinforce this link, including *Matrona*[248] (Latin for *Mother*) and *Rigana*[249] (Gallic for *Queen*).

---

[247] *Dindshenchas 4:200.*
[248] *CIL 13:5674.*

Búanann

Búanann was a warrior woman, who along with the warrior women Scáthach, was responsible for training the hero Cú Chulainn in some versions of the Wooing of Emer (*Tochmarc Emire*).

The name Búanann means *"The Lasting One"*, and is also given in a shorter form as Búan. In this shorter form there is a well named after her in Iveragh, Co. Kerry, called Búan's Well or St. Buonia's Well.

When the Morrígan offers herself to Cú Chulainn and is turned down by him, she introduces herself as *"Búan's daughter"*. In *Cormac's Glossary* we find: *"Búannan, the foster mother of the fiana, that is, the lady Anu."* Taken together all these elements strongly imply this is another guise of the Morrígan.

In the nineteenth century the writer John O'Donovan made a connection between Búanann and the Roman Goddess of War and Wisdom, Minerva.[250] A similar connection is also discussed by the classicist François Bader between the Morrígan and Athena,[251] though this is a questionable attribution.[252]

---

[249] *Textes gaulois et gallo-romains en cursive latine, II:Chamalière* – Lejeune & Marichal, 1976.

[250] *Búanann: the Minerva of the pagan Irish* – gloss from *Supplement to O'Reilly's Irish-English Dictionary*, John O'Donovan, 1864.

[251] *Rhapsodies Homériques et Irlandaises* in *Recherches sur les religions de l'antiquité classique*, Paris, 1980.

[252] Whilst it is true they are both Goddesses of War, and to an extent Wisdom, and are sometimes portrayed winged, the Morrígan has many other aspects to her character lacking in the character of Athene/Minerva, such as sexuality, magic and her connection to the earth.

Cailleach

The Cailleach Beara of Scotland, the Cailleach Bheur of Ireland and the Manx Caillagh ny Gromagh can all be seen as representations of the same Goddess. By her associated qualities this crone form appears to be a survival of the guise of Earth Goddess, associated with a variety of animals and with the seasons.

The Irish and Scottish tales of the Cailleach forming the landscape by dropping stones out of her apron clearly imply that she was an Earth Goddess. Her protection of animals, control of the weather and association with the seasons all reinforce this attribution.

The Cailleach Beara was described as having two sisters, Cailleach Bolus and Cailleach Corca Duibune, giving the triple form often associated with the Morrígan. As the Cailleach Beara she was wed to the God Lugh. The Cailleach Bheur is connected with another major Celtic deity, Bride, as the Queen of Summer who she holds captive to wash her mantle.

This contrast of the Winter Queen and Summer Queen also occurs in the tale of *The Venomous Boar of Glen Glass*, with the Cailleach being contrasted with the maiden Grainne, another Irish Goddess, but this time of the Sun.

The crone form of the Morrígan represented by the Cailleach embodies the winter, and the year's end, in the same way that the crone represents the end of a woman's life. The transformation of the Cailleach Bheur into the Maiden of Summer also demonstrates the shape-shifting ability associated with the Morrígan.

Shape-shifting occurs a number of times in the Cailleach myths. In Scottish myth she transforms into a number of birds, including cormorant, crow, eagle, gull, heron and raven. As Gyre Carling she assumes the form of a sow, the animal associated by the Celts with the Underworld Goddess.

The many forms of the Cailleach from around Britain and her myths are discussed in the earlier chapter *Wise Crone: Tales of the Cailleach*.

Cathobodua

A Romano-Celtic inscription has been found at Haute Savoie in Gaul to a Goddess called Cathobodua.[253] This name may be another name for Badbh, in her form as Catha Badbh, *"the battle crow"*.

Gallic coins have also been found depicting a horse with a crow or raven perched on the back,[254] both totemic animals of the Morrígan and clearly suggesting her worship was also conducted in Gaul (France).

[253] *Pagan Celtic Britain* – Anne Ross, 1968, p219.
[254] *The Gods of the Celts* – Miranda Green, 1986, p99.

Don

The Welsh Goddess Don, mother of the Welsh pantheon of the House of Don, seems to be the Welsh form of the Goddess Danu. Don is married to the Death God Beli, recalling Morrígan's marriage to Néit.

Don was the sister of Math, the Magic God, and had a number of children with Beli. These included her daughter, the Sky Goddess Arianhrod, and her sons, the agriculture God Amathaon, the Smith God Govannon, the Bard and Magic God Gwydyon and Nudd.

There is little recorded about this Goddess, but Don and her attributes are considered in chapter 5 *The Earth Goddess*.

Epona

The Gallic Goddess Epona (*"Divine Horse"*) is linked to both Rhiannon and Macha as the Horse Goddess. She was popular amongst Roman cavalry soldiers, and was adopted as a tutelary deity by many of them. In this context she was often shown paired with the War God Mars, in the same way that the Morrígan is with Néit. Although she may have started off as a Goddess in her own right, the similarities we show here do indicate there was cross-fertilisation of attributes.

A number of inscriptions to her by Roman soldiers have been found in the North of Britain, e.g. at Carvoran (CIL 7:747) and Auchendavy (CIL 7:1114). Statues of her have also been discovered, including a bronze statue of her seated from Wiltshire, a statuette from Colchester, and part of a helmet with her portrayed in front of a horse.

Another shared attribute is the association with birds. A fourth century tile from Roussas in Drôme, France, shows her riding on the back of a horned goose. More significantly a stela from Altrier, France shows her seated on a hose, with a raven and a hammer of Sucellos (see the entry on Nantosuelta).

The goose is a well-known as a bird associated with war, both in pre-Roman Gaul[255] and in Rome itself, as in the famous story of the guard-geese of Rome saving it from being sacked by barbarians by making a noise and waking the soldiers.

The goose and the raven are found united in several Gallic images. The first is a relief from Senlis showing a young man (or deity) with one hand raised, surrounded by ravens and geese.[256] Two of the ravens seem to be speaking into his ears, recalling the image of Odin and his ravens Hugin and Munin.

An altar from Vaison[257] and also a vase fragment from Bavai,[258] both depict a bearded man who is thought to be the God Mars, who has a

---

[255] E.g. the sanctuary at Roqueperteuse in southern France, where goose and horse symbolism are associated with war.
[256] *Recueil General des Bas-Reliefs, Statues et Bustes de la Gaule Romaine* - E. Espérandieu, 1907, 3850.
[257] *Ibid*, 306.
[258] *Poteries a Masques Prophylactiques* – M. Renard in *Latomus* 14:202-40, 1955.

raven standing on the left arm with its beak close to his ear, as if in speech, and a running goose above the head.

Titles given for Epona further reinforce this connection, should more evidence be required. Inscriptions also refer to her as *Regina* (Latin for *Queen*) and Rigana (Gallic for *Queen*), recalling the names of Rhiannon and the Morrígan.[259]

The title *Catona* (Gallic for *Battle Goddess*) is another strong piece of evidence for Epona being another guise of the Morrígan.[260] Finally the title *Atanta* (from the Gallic for *Mother*) links her to Matrona/Modron and back to the Earth Mother guise.[261]

---

[259] *CIL 3:7750* and *CIL 3:12579* for Regina, and *Textes gaulois et gallo-romains en cursive latine, II:Chamalière* – Lejeune & Marichal, 1976, p151-6.
[260] *IEW: 534.*
[261] *IEW: 71.*

Ériu

"Ériu, though it should reach a road-end. Banba, Fotla and Fea, Neman of prophetic stanzas, Danu, mother of the Gods."[262]

Together with her sisters Banba and Fotla, Ériu represented the sovereignty of Ireland, once again showing the triple motif associated with the Morrígan. The kings of Ireland wed the sisters to ensure their role as sovereigns. After the Second Battle of Moytura, Ériu weds Lugh, but then later she is referred to as the wife of Cethor MacGriene.

A description of the goddess Ériu clearly shows her connection to the Morrígan. She is described as alternating in appearance between being a beautiful woman one moment, and a grey-white crow the next moment.[263]

When the Milesians invade Ireland, they meet Ériu at Usnech of Mide. She welcomes them and praises them, telling them that the land will be theirs forever. Ériu cleverly asks the Milesians to name Ireland after her, and to this day it still bears her name as Eire.

"A gift to me, O sons of Mil and the children of Bregan, that my name may be upon this island!"

"It will be its chief name for ever," said Amergin, *"namely Ériu (Erin)."*[264]

During the battle the Milesians kill Ériu, her sisters and their husbands, demonstrating that they will now have sovereignty over the land. However the land cannot die and so neither can sovereignty. Hence we see:

"Ériu yonder, at the hands of Suirge ...Whatever the place wherein they sleep,."[265]

---

[262] *The Book of Invasions.*
[263] *Battle of Tailtiu.*
[264] *The Book of Invasions.*
[265] *The Book of Invasions.*

The key line is *"wherein they sleep"*, implying that the sovereignty embodied by Ériu is not destroyed, but recovering from the latest invasion.

Ériu is discussed in more detail in chapter 7 *The Bestower of Sovereignty*.

Fea

"Banba, Fotla, and Fea, Nemain of prophetic stanzas, Danu, mother of the Gods."[266]

"Fea and Nemain were the two wives of Néit."[267]

The name Fea is variously translated as *"death"*, *"that which causes death"*, or *"to attack"*. Fea is described as the wife of the Battle God Néit, and also as the daughter of the Fomorian God Balor. Other guises of the Morrígan are also described as being the wife of Néit, and the meaning of her name also hint at a connection.

Fea is discussed further in chapter 7 *The Lover*.

---

[266] *The Book of Invasions.*
[267] *The Book of Invasions.*

Fedelm

Fedelm is a prophetess and poetess who advises Queen Medb in the *Táin Bó Cúailnge*. When she first arrives before Queen Medb's army she is alone in a chariot. The solitary woman in a war chariot in Irish literature has been suggested as being representative of the Morrígan.

Fedelm has a weaver's beam of white bronze in the *Táin Bó Cúailnge*, and in the version in *The Book of Leinster* she is actually weaving a fringe. This emblem of weaving hints at the Weaver of Fate, which is a role of the Morrígan.

When asked who she is, Fedelm replies, *"I am Fedelm the poetess of Connaught"* (or alternatively *Síd Chrúachna* in the *Book of Leinster*, being emphatic about the otherworldly connection by giving the faery mound as her point of origin).

Queen Medb asks Fedelm if she has the power of prophecy called *imbass forosna* ("divination which illuminates"), and Fedelm answers affirmatively. This is the major focus of Fedelm's role, that she makes predictions about the outcome of battle, a familiar role.

Fedelm is also mentioned in the conversation between Cú Chulainn and the maiden Emer. They are talking in riddles using magical place and people names to confuse Emer's eavesdropping maidens. Her name occurs between other names which all refer to guises of the Morrígan, implying that she is one of these as well:

"The foam of the two steeds of Emain Macha; over the Morrigu's Garden ... over the Marrow of the Woman Fedelm ... over the Washing-place of the horses of Dea."[268]

Fedelm is discussed in more detail in chapter 11 *The Prophetess*.

---

[268] *Tochmarc Émire.*

Glaistig

The Glaistig is a type of faery found in Scotland. It is a class of being rather than a single individual, and has accreted a number of roles and abilities. Thus we see characteristics associated with the Glaistig that we would associate with the Cailleach, such as herding and being an old woman, Washer at the Ford qualities like foretelling death by the water, and forewarning old families of death like the banshee.

Her attributions are diverse and seem to have synthesised a wide range of associations. She was depicted as being very tall or small. She was said to be able to shape-shift into a variety of animal forms, including dog, foal, mare and sheep. She was said to enjoy herding sheep and cattle (like the Cailleach Bheur).

The form of the Glaistig known as the Gruagach would guard cattle, and always stayed close to water. At times she would visit houses and ask to come in and dry herself by the fire, as she would always be dripping wet.

Indeed it was believed that if offerings of milk were left out for her she would herd and look after cattle for people. She was also said to look after lonely elderly people and people of simple mind, as well as enjoying playing games with children.

The Glaistig was said to live either in a cave, or by water at fords or in a waterfall. She was also thought to wail to foretell deaths in old families, in a manner similar to the Banshee. She was usually considered invisible, but when she permitted herself to be seen she would be in faery green.

As well as Banshee attributions she has also gained mermaid ones, like the Breton Morgen. She was described as having long golden hair, which she would be seen combing whilst stretched out on a rock. In this aspect she was known as the *gruagach mhara* ("sea-maid).

There were also malicious Glaistigs, who would attack travellers at fords. These Glaistigs were considered to be members of the Fuath, the class of Scottish faeries associated with water and considered to be particularly dangerous to humans.

More detailed discussion of the Glaistig is given in chapter 12 *The Faery Queen*.

Grián

In the *Metrical Dindshenchas* Macha is linked with the Sun Goddess Grian (whose name means *"Sun"* in Irish) on two occasions. In the description of how Armagh got its name, Macha is described *"And men say that she was Grián Banchure, 'the Sun of Womanfolk'."* [269] The two are also linked in the same sentence, indicating connection, when the phrase *"bright Grián and pure Macha"* is used in a similar manuscript. [270]

Grián is described as being the sister of Áine, who we have already considered. In many instances sisterhood or a mother-daughter relationship is used to indicate different representations of the same Goddess.

We may note that Griánne means *ugliness*, which has interesting connotations in light of the ugly hag/beautiful maiden transformation found in a number of stories. She elopes with the young beautiful Diarmuid because she does not want to be with the ageing hero Finn.

Not only does she lay a geis on him to help her escape, but she lays another one on him to sleep with her. After being chased by Finn for a year and a day, hiding in megalithic tombs (known locally in Ireland as Diarmuid and Grainne's Bed),
The couple made peace with him and lived peacefully for a while, until sixteen years later. Then Diarmuid was gored by a boar and died because Finn refused to heal him.

Much of this story is echoed in the Scottish tale of Mala Lia – *"The Venomous Wild Boar of Glen Glass"*, where Griánne is Diarmaid's wife that he has eloped with, and the poisonous boar kills him as he kills it.

Another connection is found in Scottish folklore, where the Cailleach Bheur is referred to as *"the daughter of Grianan"* or *"Grianaig"* (little Sun).

---

[269] *Rennes Dindshenchas, no. 94.*
[270] *Metrical Dindshenchas, Part 4:127*

Gwrach-y-Rhybin

The Gwrach-y-Rhybin is a faery figure from Welsh folklore that shares many characteristics with the banshee. She is a hideous faery hag who haunts Welsh families, and is also associated with specific places. In appearance she is winged, has matted black hair, overlong arms, black teeth and a hooked nose.

In the manner of the Banshee, she haunts the old Welsh families, warning of death. Her favourite method was to flap her wings against the window at night and howl the name of the person who would die.[271]

It was rare for anyone to see her as she preferred to stay in the mist, but if seen by a person she would cry out as if she was lamenting the person who was going to die. For instance she would cry *"Oh my husband! My husband!"* if a man was due to die.[272]

The Gwrach-y-Rhybin is also said to haunt Pennard Castle and the banks of the river Dribble. She has another form, known as the *yr Hen Chrwchwd* ("old hump-backed one"), in which she appears as a shrieking old woman, her cries foretelling the death of a local person.[273]

The Gwrach-y-Rhybin is discussed in more detail chapter 10 *The Washer at the Ford.*

[271] *British Goblins: Welsh Folklore, Fairy Mythology, Legends and Traditions* – Wirt Sikes, 1880, p216-7.
[272] *Ibid.*
[273] *Folklore of Wales* – Anne Ross, Stroud, 2001, p100.

Gyre Carling

The Scottish Gyre Carling has qualities associated with the Scottish Cailleach Bheur and also the English Black Annis. She carries an iron club, which we can equate with the rod of winter carried by the Cailleach Bheur. When she is attacked by dogs she shape-shifts into a pig, demonstrating another of the abilities associated with the Goddess. She also eats human flesh, which is a quality more associated with Black Annis.

She was described in private correspondence by Sir Walter Scott as the *"mother witch of the Scottish peasantry"*. In the correspondence Scott quoted the following lines from a poem in the Bannatyne MSS describing her unpleasant tastes:

*"Thair dwelt ane grit Gyre Carling in awld Betokis bour,
That levit [lived] upoun menis flesche [men's flesh]."*

This aspect of the Cailleach Bheur is discussed in chapter 3: *The Cailleach: Tales of the Wise Crone.*

Lamia

"Eyed like a peacock, and all crimson barr'd;
And full of silver moons, that, as she breathed,
Dissolv'd, or brighter shone, or interwreathed
Their lustres with the gloomier tapestries-
So rainbow-sided, touch'd with miseries,
She seem'd, at once, some penanced lady elf,
Some demon's mistress, or the demon's self."[274]

The ninth century Irish writer Cormac describes the Badbh as *Lamia*, which gives a suggestion that the three Lamiae at the Roman fort of Benwell[275] in Northern Britain could be a depiction of the Morrígan as the War Goddess in her triple form (particularly with the references in early Glossaries to the connection between the two, with Badb being glossed for Lamia).

The inscription says *Lamiis Tribus*, meaning "to the three Lamiae". The popular image of the Lamia certainly bears similarity to a number of Morrígan attributes, and some sources also describe the lamiae as a type of faery.

"When Apollonius and his companions travailed in a bright Moone shine night, they saw a certaine apparition of Phairies, in latine called Lamia, and in greek Empusa, changing themselves from one shape into another, being also sometimes visible, and presently vanishing out of sight againe."[276]

---

[274] *Lamia* – John Keats (1795-1821), 1820.
[275] *CIL (Corpus Inscriptionum Latinarum),7:507* , Berlin, 1862.
[276] *The Historie of Foure-Footed Beastes* – Edward Topsell, 1607.

Mab

Queen Mab is best known for her appearance in Shakespeare's *Romeo and Juliet.* Here the Faery Queen has been reduced to a tiny figure, belittling the power of otherworldly beings. Queen Medb of the Irish myths has become Queen Mab, but in a substantially reduced form.

Both characters share a number of characteristics that indicate this commonality. As well as the similarity of their names, they are both fiercely independent queens, and are both highly sexual. In his speech in the play, Mercutio makes a number of references which seem to substantiate the derivation of Mab from Medb, and hence ultimately the Morrígan.

The first obvious connection is the horse link, for Shakespeare says *"This is that very Mab that plats the manes of horses in the night."*[277] Even though she is very small, Mab is still given the appropriate means of travel, *"Her chariot is an empty hazel-nut."*[278] Although the chariot is small, still she rides it alone, in the manner of the Warrior Queen, and additionally the chariot is made from hazel, representing wisdom in the Celtic myths.

He also refers to her saying, *"This is the hag".*[279] This reminds us of the hag/maiden Bestower of Sovereignty found repeatedly in tales linked to the Morrígan.

Ben Jonson continued the legend of Queen Mab, writing of her in his *Entertainment of the Queen and Prince at Althrope* in 1603. He refers to several of the associated qualities of the Faery folk, showing the common views of his time. Mab influences dreams, robs the dairy, pinches wenches and steals children.

Mab is discussed in more detail in chapter 12 *The Faery Queen.*

---

[277] *Romeo and Juliet* I:4.
[278] *Romeo and Juliet* I:4.
[279] *Romeo and Juliet* I:4.

Mala Lia

"His lair on Meall-an-Tuirc's rough side
Where Mala Lia' kept her swine –
Witch Mala Lia', evil-eyed,
Foul, shapeless and malign –
Was all begrimed with filth and gore
And horrid with the limbs of men
The unclean monster killed and tore
To feast on in his den."[280]

In the tale of *The Venomous Boar of Glen Glass*, the hero Diarmaid hunts the deadly wild boar. Here the Cailleach is referred to as *Mala Liath* (Grey Eyebrows) and is the protectress of swine. Nobody had managed to kill the boar, but Diarmaid tracks it to its lair. On his way to its lair a raven pecking a hare's corpse and a crow on a boulder both warn him off.

The raven tells him that he will kill the boar but die in the process, and the crow does the same, telling him to return to his wife Grainne. Mala Lia follows Diarmaid, taunting him and cursing him, urging him to return to Grainne. In reply Diarmaid throws her over a cliff and fights the boar. He kills it but in doing so is slain by a venomous bristle, which pierces the inside of one of his heels.

This tale suggests earlier roots, with the choice between the old crone of winter Mala Lia and the maiden of summer Grainne. Mala Lia tries in vain to persuade Diarmaid to return to his summer maiden, appearing as both a crow and a raven, foretelling his death, reminding us of the Morrígan trying to save Cú Chulainn. But like Cú Chulainn, Diarmaid is headstrong and will not listen to her, and pays the price by dying after fighting the poisonous boar.

This aspect of the Cailleach Bheur is discussed in more detail in chapter 3 *The Cailleach: Tales of the Wise Crone*.

---

[280] *The Venomous Wild Boar of Glen Glass* – Dr. Arthur Sutherland, in *The Highland Monthly*, 1892, vol 4:491.

Medb

Queen Medb (*"Drunk Woman"* or *"The Intoxicating One"*[281]) is a Warrior Queen who shows the skills and appetites associated with the Morrígan. Her name is often anglicized to Maeve, and it is likely that the Faery Queen Mab was derived from her. She could run faster than the swiftest horse (like Macha), and sight of her deprived men of two thirds of their strength. It was Medb who was the great rival of Cú Chulainn. Medb led the forces with the Children of Cailitín that finally kill Cú Chulainn.

Medb is described in the *Táin* in a manner that implies her faery and otherworldly connection. She is *"a woman, tall, beautiful, pale and long faced. She had flowing, golden-yellow hair. She wore a crimson, hooded cloak with a golden brooch over her breast. A straight, ridged spear blazing in her hand."*[282]

Medb is clearly a sovereignty figure, as all her husbands become kings. Thus she is married to Conchobar (King of Ulster), who she forsakes due to "pride of mind", then Tinne (King of Connacht). After Eochaid is killed by Conchobar, who subsequently rapes her,[283] she takes Eochaid Dala as her husband (who becomes King of Connacht with Medb's consent). By the time of the Táin she has married her fourth husband, Ailill mac Mata.

Medb is also the cause of the battle that forces Cú Chulainn to kill his friend Fer Diad, for it is her desire to see the two great bulls (the Brown Bull and the White-horned Bull) fight, and the oath she swears to this end, which results in the Táin.[284] As this is caused by the cries of the calf that was the result of the Morrígan's cattle-stealing activities we again see her hand in this.

Another parallel to the behaviour of the Morrígan may be seen in Medb's advice to Cú Chulainn. Her champions are reluctant to fight him due to his youth, so Medb sends a message to him to stain his

---

[281] In this context it is interesting to note that the word *mead* comes from the same root.
[282] *Táin Bó Cúailnge.*
[283] This is suggested as being the initial cause of the *Táin*, and indicates an attempt to take the sovereignty by force, a fact that causes war as the other kings are not happy about this.
[284] *Echtra Nerai.*

face with blackberry juice so they will fight him. Cú Chulainn does so, and then fights Lóch and kills him, despite the interference of the Morrígan.

Medb is a great warrior and also has an insatiable sexual appetite, sleeping with thirty men a day. In one story she sleeps with Cú Chulainn,[285] and offers her thighs in exchange for the loan of the Brown Bull, she sleeps with the hero Fergus to gain his assistance, and also entices Fer Diad to fight Cú Chulainn for her.

She also had many children, in the fashion of a Fertility Goddess. Medb refers to the otherworldly colours of white and red when talking to her husband Ailill about the bride-price she gave him, emphasising her otherworldliness: *"The breadth of your face in red gold, the weight of your left arm in white bronze."*[286]

The last consideration is one that demonstrates Medb's divine power in an unusual manner. When her army is retreating, Medb's bleeding begins and she needs to urinate. Menstrual blood and urine both have long histories as symbols of sexual potency, and also as protective substances. Medb uses this to cover her retreat:

"Then her issue of blood came upon Medb (and she said: "O Fergus, cover) the retreat of the men of Ireland that I may pass my water" ... *Medb passed her water and it made three great trenches in each of which a household can fit."*[287]

Medb also asked Cú Chulainn who had approached whilst she urinated, but would not strike her from behind, to cover the retreat of her army. He agreed and protected the enemy army, much to the annoyance of his own side. This is not a rational action unless there is more going on here than meets the eye, i.e. Medb is a Goddess.

In another tale[288] Medb again urinates when retreating, but in this instance the urine has a destructive quality on the land, for *"neither root nor underbrush nor stick of wood was left .... And neither root nor growth nor grass, in its pure, lovely ripeness, was left in that place forever after"*

---

[285] *Fled Bicrenn.*
[286] *Táin Bó Cúailnge.*
[287] *The Book of Leinster.*
[288] *Táin Bó Flidaise II.*

The Gallic river Goddess Meduana, (*the Intoxicatress*) referred to at hot springs near Trier,[289] may be another form of Medb, emphasising the water aspect of the Goddess.

---

[289] *CIL* 13:7667.

Modron

Although she is mentioned only briefly in the *Mabinogion*, there is an argument for a link between this Goddess and the Morrígan as well. The name Modron is derived from Matrona ("Great Mother"), who is suggested as a sovereignty figure.[290]

The children of Modron and her husband Urien are Owein and Morfydd. Owein is best known for his game of chess with King Arthur in *The Dream of Rhonabwy*.[291] During this chess game Arthur's men start slaying Owein's ravens, but as the game proceeds the tables are turned and the ravens slay many of Arthur's men. This raven motif is highly reminiscent of the Morrígan.

Another Welsh tale referring to the *"Ford of Barking"*[292] also brings several of these figures together with Morrígan themes.[293] In this tale Urien goes to the ford to discover why the dogs have stopped barking. He finds a woman washing there (i.e. the Washer at the ford). They have sex (reminiscent of the union of the Morrígan and the Daghda), and she tells him that she is the daughter of the King of Annwn[294] and if he returns in a year she will present him with a child.

When he returns he is presented with twins – Owein and Morfydd. This thus links Modron as the mother of these children in *The Mabinogion* with the Washer at the Ford and completes the argument that Modron is another guise of the Morrígan.

---

[290] *Morgan le Fee and Celtic Goddesses* - R.S. Loomis, 1940, p194
[291] From *The Mabinogion*.
[292] Rhyd y Gyfartha.
[293] *MSS Peniarth 147*, c. 1556.
[294] The underworld in Welsh myth.

Morgan Le Fay

The name Morgan Le Fay translates as "born of the sea", and Morrígan can mean "Sea Queen". Additionally the magical powers of Morgan Le Fay and her otherworldly connections, also suggest a guise of the Morrígan.

Further parallels can be seen by Morgan's association with the otherworldly island of Avalon, corresponding to Scáthach's otherworldly island of Dún Scaith. Her name of Le Fay (*"the faery"*) also implies a link to the Morrígan as the Faery Queen.

The first occurrence of Morgan in *Vita Merlini* in 1150 already shows her having a number of powers attributed to the Morrígan, as well as being one of nine sisters, a significant Morrígan number.

"That is the place where nine sisters exercise a kindly rule over those who come to them from our land. The one who is first among them has greater skill in healing, as her beauty surpasses that of her sisters. Her name is Morgen, and she has learned the uses of all plants in curing the ills of the body. She knows, too, the art of changing her shape, of flying through the air."[295]

The love-hate relationship between Morgan Le Fay and King Arthur is also very reminiscent of the relationship between the Morrígan and Cú Chulainn. For although she has tried to cause his downfall, it is also Morgan Le Fay who is in the barge as one of the three queens who takes the mortally wounded Arthur to the Isle of Avalon to be healed.

The other queens are the Queen of Northgalis (North Wales) and the Queen of the Wastelands. As Morgan was married to the Welsh King Uriens it is possible these other two queens are representations of her, showing the triple motif often associated with the Morrígan.

The literary presence of Morgan Le Fay and her qualities are covered in more detail in chapter 13 *Morgan Le Fay and the Arthurian Mythos.*

---

[295] *Vita Merlini.*

Muilidheartach

"There were two slender spears of battle upon either side of the hag; her face was blue-black, the lustre of coal and her bone tufted tooth was like rusted bone. In her head was one deep pool-like eye swifter than a star in a winter sky; upon her head gnarled brushwood like the clawed old wood of aspen root."[296]

The Muilidheartach[297] appears to be a watery form of the Scottish Cailleach Bheur. When in the water her description is reptilian. However she could also assume the form of a hag, who could raise winds and sea-storms (like Black Annis). Her description is entirely in keeping with descriptions of aspects of the Morrígan, particularly Badb.

The Muilidheartach is one of the Fuath, i.e. a dangerous water faery. She would appear as a hag at the door, dripping wet and begging to be allowed to dry herself by the fire. If she was refused she would grow in size and ferocity and make the unfortunate person regret their refusal.[298]

---

[296] *Popular Tales of the West Highlands* – J.F. Campbell, 1860, p125
[297] Pronounced "moolyarstuch".
[298] *Scottish Folk-Lore and Folk Life* – Donald MacKenzie, 1935.

Nantosuelta

The Gallic Goddess Nantosuelta, whose name means "Winding River", also has elements of commonality with the Morrígan suggesting a link. The Morrígan is often found associated with bodies of water, especially rivers, as fords are one of her power places as the Washer at the Ford.

She is partnered with Sucellos ("the Good Striker"), a War God in the same way that the Morrígan is partnered with Néit. It is also worth observing that Sucellos with his hammer and cauldron also bears a strong resemblance to the Daghda with his club and cauldron.

The raven is the main symbol of Nantosuelta, again making a connection to the Morrígan, along with the dovecote, indicating a more domestic aspect. She is also sometimes depicted with a cornucopia (horn of plenty), indicating a bountiful Earth Goddess aspect.

A small carved stone found in East Stoke in Nottinghamshire (England) is thought to represent Nantosuelta, suggesting the worship of this guise of the Morrígan may have traveled.

Rhiannon

A number of scholars have taken the view that Rhiannon is a counterpart of Macha,[299] and also Epona. Macha is linked to horses through being able to outrun any of them. In the case of Rhiannon she has a horse that can outrun any horse without even breaking sweat, and subsequently has to take the role of a horse carrying people as punishment for the crime she did not commit.

The name Rhiannon is derived from Rigatona, meaning *"Great Queen"*, which is one of the translations of Morrígan. The birds of Rhiannon are able to wake the dead and cause the living to sleep,[300] bringing the psychopomp aspect of the Morrígan to mind as well as her avian connection.

Rhiannon is also a Sovereignty Goddess associated with the faery. In the tale *Pwyll Prince of Dyved*[301] her faery association is indicated both by her being initially seen on a mound (faery dwelling) and also riding a pure white horse indicating her divine and regal status. Both these characteristics associate her with the land.

Another association with the land is the bag she gives Pwyll that he fills with food but is never full. This is akin to a reverse cornucopia or horn of plenty. After their union Rhiannon gives away a huge quantity of rich gifts to all who ask, indicating her bountiful nature.

After Pwyll's death, Rhiannon marries the God of Wisdom and the Sea, Manawyddan. She is subsequently turned into an ass by Llwyd to avenge his friend's son for the harm done to him by Pwyll. Manawyddan outwits Llwyd and Rhiannon is restored to human form, but once again we see the horse attribution to her in this story.[302]

See also chapter 7 *The Bestower of Sovereignty* for more discussion of connections between Rhiannon and the Morrígan.

---

[299] See particularly *Epona-Rhiannon-Macha* – Jean Gricourt, in Ogam 31:25-40, 137-8; 32:75-86; 34:165-88; 36:269-72, 1954; and *Macha and Conall Cernach: A Study of Two Iconographic Patterns in Medieval Irish Narratives and Celtic Art* – Paula Powers Coe, 1995, p95-99 and 120-33.
[300] See *Branwen the Daughter of Lyr* in *The Mabinogion*.
[301] In *The Mabinogion*.
[302] See *Manawyddan the Son of Llyr* in *The Mabinogion*.

Scáthach

After his early experiences Cú Chulainn goes off to the mysterious island of Scáthach (which means *"the shadowy one"*) called Dún Scaith (the island of Skye) for training as a warrior. This he must do to win the hand of Emer, daughter of Forgall Manach. His training and experiences there are described in *Tochmarc Emire*.

Scáthach demonstrates a number of qualities that suggest her as another guise of the Morrígan. Her otherworldly island that can only be reached by a difficult journey is an obvious sign. The meaning of both her name and that of her daughter, Úathach *("spectre")* are also indicators.

Scáthach's ability as a warrior, and her ability to prophesy also show that she possesses qualities we associate particularly with the Morrígan, and her prophecy to Cú Chulainn in *Verba Scáthaige* before he leaves is one of the major predictions of the whole myth cycle.

The triple motifs which abound in this encounter also indicate the presence of the Morrígan. After three days Úathach tells Cú Chulainn the three demands he must make of Scáthach. During his time with Scáthach, Cú Chulainn fights the warrior woman Aífe. He bests her and makes three demands of her: that she gives hostages to Scáthach, that she spend the night with him, and that she bears him a son. She agrees and does all three.

Scáthach teaches Cú Chulainn the arts of the warrior, including the mighty salmon leap, and the use of the deadly Gae Bolga spear, which is thrown with the feet, as one might expect from a Battle Goddess.

Valkyries

The obvious commonalities between the Morrígan and the Norse Valkyries have been recorded many times. Some writers have suggested that some Celtic influences cross-fertilised the way the Valkyries are portrayed in Norse sagas.[303]

Let us consider these similarities so that you can make up your own mind. The Valkyries ride their horses through the air, over land and sea, and conduct the chosen fallen warrior heroes to Valhalla. The name Valkyries means *"choosers of the slain".*[304] The Morrígan is also linked to horses and chooses her pick of the fallen warriors, i.e. both act as the psychopomp.

The individual Valkyries have a wide range of names, as they are a class of being. They revel in war[305] but may also provide supernatural aid to warriors.[306] An example of the latter form of aid that completely duplicates the actions of the Morrígan is the striking terror into the hearts of the enemy.[307]

The Valkyries prophesy the outcome of battles and determine it, both by supernatural and physical intervention.[308] All these behavioural characteristics are indicative of War Goddesses, and again all these qualities can be seen in the behaviour of the Morrígan in the various Irish tales.

The Morrígan is particularly linked to the corvid family, frequently appearing as a crow or raven. Whilst the Valkyries are commonly linked with swans, they also do appear on occasions as crows as well.[309] It is also worth noting that the Old English term *wælceasiga*

---

[303] E.g. *Studien zur germanischen Sagengeschichte: Der Valkyrjenmythus* – Wolfgang Golther, Munich, 1888 and *Le Cygne et la Valkyrie: Dévaluation d'un mythe* – Jéré,ie Benoit, Paris, 1989.
[304] From the Old Norse *val* meaning "battlefield carnage" and *kjósa* meaning "to choose".
[305] E.g. *Víga-Glúms Saga 21:78-85* and *Njáls Saga 454-58*.
[306] This even results in marriage in some sagas.
[307] E.g. *Hromundar saga Greidssonar* where Kara sings spells preventing the enemy from acting.
[308] E.g. *Gylfaginning 36, Hromundar Saga, Volsunga Saga*.
[309] E.g. In *Volsunga Saga* where a Valkyrie delivers an apple from Odin to Rerir in the form of a crow.

meaning "the slain-choosing one" translates exactly to the Old Norse *valkyrja*.

The Valkyries often become lovers and sometimes even brides to heroes they have aided and saved on the battlefield. Macha Mongruad fights and defeats the male competitors for kingship, and then marries one of them, in a manner reminiscent of the Valkyries choice.

Finally although they may partner off with mortal heroes they love, Valkyries tended to end up being the instruments of those same heroes' deaths, in the same way that the Morrígan ends up being the instrument of Cú Chulainn's death.

Appendixes

i) From Cailleach to Sheela-na-gig?

A number of modern writers have suggested the development of the Sheela-na-gig figures found over church doorways from the crone figure of the Cailleach.[310] If this is the case then perhaps the Morrígan did manage to infiltrate the Christian Church or be assimilated in one of her guises.

The name Sheela-na-gig is suggested as coming from the Gaelic *síle-na-glíoch*. This word may come either from *Sighe na gCioch* meaning *old hag of the paps*, or *Síle na Giob* meaning *Sheela on her hunkers* (i.e. squatting). In both these cases we can see that the name begins with *Sí*, the word for faery.

The first examples of Sheela-na-gig figures come from eleventh century French churches. We already know that guises of the Morrígan existed in France from much earlier than this, so the derivation is a possible one. The first of these figures to reach Ireland did so during the 1160s.

The physical image of the Sheela-na-gig certainly reminds us of aspects of the Morrígan. She is usually portrayed as being a very ugly hag. The Morrígan often appears in this guise, as Badb, the Cailleach, etc. The tales are full of descriptions appropriate to these carvings.

The displaying of the genitals to emphasise sexuality is another appropriate symbolism for the Morrígan. The squatting woman is highly reminiscent of the image of Queen Medb urinating when she has her courses.

The gaping genitalia bring to mind the opening to the primal womb, often represented in the past as caves and chambers in mounds. In this context the faery association springs back to mind, with the *Sídh* or faery mound as the otherworld entered by the dark tunnel. To this end the fact that Sheela-na-gigs are placed over doors to churches, (or sometimes over doorways in castles) symbolising the entrance to "another realm", i.e. the place of worship, is highly significant.

---

[310] E.g. Lisa M. Bitel in *Land of Women: Tales of Sex and Gender from Early Ireland*, Anne Ross - *The Divine Hag of the Pagan Celts* in *The Witch Figure*, Lorraine Kochanske Stock in *The Hag of Castle Hautdesert: The Celtic Sheela-na-gig and the Auncian in Sir Gawain and the Green Knight*.

An apotropaic function is often suggested for Sheela-na-gigs, functioning like gargoyles as protective grotesques that keep away evil. This brings to mind the whole tradition of the "loathly lady", who embodies the sovereignty of the land, and is transformed into a beautiful maiden by the true candidate for kingship.

A thirteenth century romance about the popular hero Gawain has him attacked by a figure whose description sounds remarkably like not only a sovereignty hag but also a Sheela-na-gig.[311]

"Her ostrich eyes burned like fire; her nose was hideous – wondrously broad and flat ... the wide, thick-lipped mouth turned up towards the ears, and from it protruded sharp, broad teeth that met in four places like a boar's ... The wrinkled jowls of the devilish woman hung down to her chin ... The hands and arms of the wild woman were fully as strong as pillars; she had long claws that were sharp and powerful ... Below the waist, around the pelvis, she resembled nothing but an ape, and the place below was hideous, looking like a horse collar.[312] Her skin hung on her as wrinkled and folded as a sack, while her sinews beneath were as large as wagon ropes."[313]

---

[311] *Diu Krône* – Heinrich von dem Türlin.
[312] Note the emphasis on the large genitalia.
[313] *Diu Krône.*

ii) A Possible Lacnunga Reference

The classic Anglo-Saxon healing book commonly known as the Lacnunga[314] contains an intriguing reference that may refer to the warrior aspect of the Morrígan. The manuscript was written in Old English around 1000. The reference in question is in paragraph 135, which begins as follows:

"Loud they were, lo, loud when they rode over the burial-mound; they were fierce when they rode over the land … I stood under the linden-wood, under a light shield where the mighty women put forth their powers and sent their yelling spears."

The first significant component that draws the attention is reference to the *burial-mound*, which is a classic entrance to the otherworld, associated with the faery folk. That the women are *mighty* and also armed with *yelling spears* also brings the Morrígan to mind.

The text refers to wounds from missile weapons, including elf-shot. Thus the text distinguishes between them, saying *"Out spear, be not in spear"* referring to normal spears, and also *"Out little spear if it be in here"* referring to elf-shot.[315]

To be safe the text also gives several classes of being who can enchant missile weapons, to protect against all of them. It is interesting to note that these types of being are Gods, faery and witches.

---

[314] *MSS Harley 585*, British Library
[315] "Little spear" was a commonly used term to describe elf-shot.

iii) The Morrígan and Flint Arrowheads

Flint arrowheads (also known as *glossopetrae*) were believed in the Middle Ages to be the fossilised tongues of serpents. When mounted in silver[316] they were thought to be an effective charm to protect cattle from fairy and elf bewitchments, a practice that continued until recent times in Ireland.

Considering the use of the arrowhead (war) to protect cattle (sacred to her) from bewitchments (her field of expertise) or faery (her court) - this strongly hints of the Morrígan.

There was also a tradition in Middle Age Ireland that if a woman found a flint arrowhead she would be elevated to the position of village medical counselor, due to the ascribed properties of the arrowhead.

This ascension to a form of sovereignty concerned with growth and well-being reinforces the idea that this may have been a continuation of the tradition of honouring the power of the wise-woman as the representative of the Morrígan, echoing her earlier roles as Earth Goddess and Bestower of Sovereignty.

The arrowhead would be soaked in water and the water given to the afflicted person to drink.[317] This water was also thought to heal cows and horses that had been wounded by "elf shot" or "elf darts".

A nineteenth century English literary reference also hints at a connection between the Morrígan (as the Cailleach) and elf-shot. In the classic *Wuthering Heights*,[318] a delirious Cathy Earnshaw abuses her hostile housekeeper, saying:

"I see in you, Nelly, an aged woman; you have grey hair and bent shoulders.[319] This bed is the fairy cave under Peniston Crag and you are gathering elf-bolts to hurt our heifers,[320] pretending while I am near, that they are only locks of wool."

---

[316] These silver-mounted arrowheads were known as *saigead*.

[317] See comments elsewhere regarding the magical nature of water and its connection to the Morrígan

[318] *Wuthering Heights* - Emily Bronte (1818-1848), 1847.

[319] A clear allusion to the elderly Cailleach.

[320] Note the reference to the fairy cave. Elf-bolt is another name for elf-shot.

Taken together, all the symbols and uses of the flint arrowheads can be seen as being potentially symbolic of the Morrígan, a tribute to her power to endure in the hearts and spirits of the people even during Christian rule.

iv) Celtic Raven Lore

The inherently magical nature of the corvid family is found repeatedly throughout Celtic myth and folklore. Apart from the connection to the Goddess Morrígan, there are various other interesting aspects that may ultimately be derived from this association.

Augury

Many people are familiar with the children's Magpie rhyme, but do not realise it is a survival of old folklore. Likewise there is also a rhyme about ravens, giving different auguries (omens) by the number of ravens you sight when you are out and about in nature.

One for bad news, Two for mirth.
Three is a wedding, Four is a birth.
Five is for riches, Six is a thief.
Seven, a journey, Eight is for grief.
Nine is a secret, Ten is for sorrow.
Eleven is for love, Twelve - joy for tomorrow.

Harbingers

Ravens are well known as birds of omen. References are found throughout the examples already given in this book. However we may also mention passages in *The Lay of the Wife of Meargach*[321] which demonstrate reading of both the cry and flight of the raven:-

"I knew by the voice of the raven, each morning since you journeyed from me, that your downfall was true and certain, and that you would not return to the land victorious."

"I knew on looking after you the day on which you travelled from the fort, by the flight of the raven going forth before you that it was no propitious sign of your return to me.

---

[321] Translated in *Ossianic Society* 4:173.

Moreover, a skilled person could read the calls of the raven to divine exactly what they were saying. The following piece from a Middle Irish codex (Trinity H.3.17)[322] gives detail of this.

"If the raven call from above an enclosed bed in the midst of the house, it is a distinguished grey-haired guest or clerics that are coming to you, but there is a difference between them. If it be a lay-cleric the raven says "bacach"; if it be a man in orders it says "gradh gradh" and twice in the day it calls. If it be warrior guests or satirists that are coming, it is "gracc gracc" it calls, or "grob grob", and it calls in the quarter behind you, and it is from there the guests are coming. If it calls "gracc gracc" the warriors to whom it calls are oppressed. If woman are coming it calls long. If it calls from the north-east end of the house, robbers are about to steal the horses. If it calls from the house door, strangers or soldiers are coming. If it calls from above the door, satirists or guests from a king's retinue are coming. If it calls from above the goodman's bed, the place where his weapons will be, and he going on a journey, he will not come back safe, but if not, he will come back sound. If it is the woman who is about to die, it is from the pillow it calls. If it call from the foot of the man's bed his son or brother or his son-in-law will come to the house. If it call from the edge of the storehouse where the food is kept, there will be increase of food from the quarter it calls, that is flesh-meat or first milking of kine. If its face be between the storehouse and the fire, agreeable guests are coming to the house. If it be near to the woman of the house, where her seat is, the guests are for her, namely, a son-in-law or a friend. If it call from the south of the storehouse, fosterage or guests from afar are coming to the house. If it speak with a small voice, that is "err err" or "ur ur", sickness will fall on some one in the house, or on some of the cattle. If wolves are coming amongst the sheep, it is from the sheep-fold it calls, or from over against the good women, and what it says is "carna, carna" [flesh, flesh], "grob, grob, coin, coin" [wolves, wolves]. If it calls from the rooftree of the house when people are eating, they throw away that food. If it call from a high tree, then it is death-tidings of a young lord. If it calls from a stone it is death-tidings of an aithech. If it go with thee on a journey or in front of you, and if it be joyful, your journey will prosper and fresh meat will be given to you. If you come left-hand-wise and it calls before you, he is a doomed man on whom it calls thus, or it is the wounding of some one of the company. If it be before you when going to an assembly, there will be an uprising therein. If it be left-hand-

---

[322] *Prognostications from the Raven and the Wren* – R.I. Best in *Ériu* 8:120.

wise it has come, some one is slain in that uprising. If it call from the corner where the horses are, robbers are about to attack them. If it then turn on its back and says "grob, grob", some of the horses will be stolen and they will not be recovered."

Poisonous Flesh

The flesh of the raven was often believed to be poisonous if eaten. Not only this, but it possesses malefic powers for use in negative magic. Hence we see there is an old Scottish belief that people could be killed by referring to this by shaking a bridle at them and reciting the spell *"raven's flesh and crane's flesh come out of thy way"*.[323]

---

[323] *The Church of Alves* – W. Cramond, 1900.

Bibliography

Abbot, T.K., Catalogue of the Manuscripts in the Library of Trinity College, Dublin, 1900, Hodges Figgis & Co, Dublin

Andersen, Jørgen, The Witch on the Wall: Medieval Erotic Sculpture in the British Isles, 1977, Rosenkilde & Bagger, Copenhagen

d'Arbois de Jubainville, H., Étude sur le Táin Bó Cúalnge autrement dit "Enlèvement des vaches de Cooley", 1907, in Revue Celtique 28:17-40

---------, Enlèvement du taureau divin et des vaches de Cooley, 1908, trans, in Revue Celtique 28:145-77, 28:241-61; 29:153-201; 30:78-88, 30:156-85

Archdeacon, Matthew, Legends of Connaught, 1839, Dublin

Arthurs, M.J.B., Macha and Armagh, Bulletin of the Ulster Place Name Society 1:25-9

Bader, Françoise, Rhapsodies Homériques et Irlandaises, 1980, in Recherches sur les religions de l'antiquité classique, Librairie Champion, Paris

Barden, Patrick, The Dead-Watchers and Other Folk-Lore Tales of Westmeath, 1891, Mullingar

Baudis, J., CúRói and CúChulainn, 1914, in Ériu 7:200-09

Beattie, William (ed), Border Ballads, 1952, Penguin Books Ltd, Edinburgh

Bellows, Henry A. (trans), The Poetic Edda, 1936, Princeton University Press, Princeton

Benoit, F., L'Heroisation Equestre, 1954, Aix-en-Provence

Best, R.I., Prognostications from the Raven and the Wren, 1916, in Ériu 8:120.

Best, R.I. & Bergin, Osborn (eds), Lebor na huidre: Book of the Dun Cow, 1929, Royal Irish Academy, Dublin

Best, R.I. & O'Brien, M.A. (eds), The Book of Leinster (Volume 2), 1956, Dublin Institute for Advanced Studies, Dublin

---------, The Book of Leinster (Volume 4), 1965, Dublin Institute for Advanced Studies, Dublin

---------, The Book of Leinster (Volume 5), 1967, Dublin Institute for Advanced Studies, Dublin

Bhreathnach, M., The Sovereignty Goddess as Goddess of Death?, 1982, in Zeitschrift für Celtische Philologie 39:243-60

Billson, Charles James, County Folk-Lore Printed Extracts No.3: Leicestershire & Rutland, 1895, David Nutt, London

Bitel, Lisa M., Land of Women: Tales of Sex and Gender from Early Ireland, 1996, Cornell University Press, Ithaca

Boece, Hector, The Chronicles of Scotland, 1936, The Scottish Texts Society, Edinburgh

Bowen, Charles, Great-Bladdered Medb: Mythology and Invention in the Táin Bó Cúailnge, 1975, in Eire-Ireland 10:14-34

---------, A Historical Inventory of the Dindshenchas, 1975/6, in Studia Celtica 10-11:113-37

Breatnach, R.A., The Lady and the King: A Theme of Irish Literature, 1953, in Studies: An Irish Quarterly Review 42:321-36

Briggs, Katharine, *A Dictionary of Fairies*, 1976, Penguin Books, London
Bronte, Emily, *Wuthering Heights*, 1991, Running Press, New York
Bruford, A., *Gaelic Folk-Tales and Medieval Romances*, 1966, Dublin
Byock, Jesse (trans), *The Saga of King Hrolf Kraki*, 1998, Penguin Books Ltd, London
Byrne, F.J., *Irish Kings and High Kings*, 1973, B.T. Batsford Ltd, London
Caesar, Caius Julius, *The Gallic War*, 1917, William Heinemann, London
Calder, G. (ed), *Togail na Tebe: The Thebaid of Statius*, 1922, Cambridge
Campbell, J.F., *Popular Tales of the West Highlands* (4 volumes), 1860, Alexander Gardner, London
---------, *The Scottish Historical Review* Volume 12, 1915, 4:413
Campbell, John G., *Superstitions of the Highlands & Islands of Scotland*, 1900, MacLehose & Sons, Glasgow
---------, *Witchcraft and Second Sight in the Highlands & Islands of Scotland*, 1902, MacLehose & Sons, Glasgow
Carey, John, *The Name Túatha Dé Danann*, 1980-1, in *Éigse* 18:291-94
---------, *Notes on the Irish War Goddess*, 1982-3, in *Éigse* 19:263-75
---------, *The Irish "Otherworld"*, 1991, in *Éigse* 25:154-9
Carmichael, Alexander (ed), *Carmina Gadelica*, 1992, Lindisfarne Books
Carney, James, *Studies in Irish Literature and History*, 1955, Dublin Institute for Advanced Studies, Dublin
Cassius, Dio, *Dio's Roman History* (9 volumes), 1924, William Heinemann, London
Chadwick, N.K., *Imbas Forosnai*, 1935, in *Scottish Gaelic Studies IV 2:97-135*
Chaucer, Geoffrey, *Canterbury Tales*, 1996, Penguin Books Ltd, London
CIL, *Corpus Inscriptionum Latinarum*, 1862, Akademie der Wissenschaften
Clark, Rosalind, *The Great Queens: Irish Goddesses from the Morrígan to Cathleen Ní Houlihan*, 1991, Irish Literary Studies 34, Colin Smythe, Gerrards Cross
Clarke, Basil, *The Life of Merlin*, 1973, Cardiff University Press, Cardiff
Coe, Paula Powers, *Macha and Conall Cernach: A Study of Two Iconographic Patterns in Medieval Irish Narratives and Celtic Art*, 1995, Dissertation, UCLA, Los Angeles
Collingwood, R.G. & Wright, P.G. (eds), *The Roman Inscriptions of Britain*, 1965, Clarendon Press, Oxford
Colum, P. (ed), *A Treasury of Irish Folklore*, 1954, New York
Condren, Mary, *The Serpent and the Goddess: Women, Religion and Power in Celtic Ireland*, 1989, Harper & Row, San Francisco
Cooney, Gabriel, *Sacred and Secular Neolithic Landscapes in Ireland*, in *Sacred Sites, Sacred Places*, 1994, Routledge, London
Corthals, John, *The Rhetoric in Aided Chonchobbuir*, 1989, in *Ériu* 40:41-59
Cramond, W., *The Church of Alves*, 1900, Elgin
Cross, Tom Peete, & Slover, Clark Harris, *Ancient Irish Tales*, 1936, Barnes & Noble, New York
Curry, Eugene, *Cath Mhuighe Léana, or The Battle of Magh Leana*, 1855, Celtic Society, Dublin
Dalton, G.F., *The "Loathly Lady": A Suggested Interpretation*, in *Folklore* 82:124-31, 1971

Davidson, H.R. Ellis, *Myths and Symbols in Pagan Europe: Early Scandinavian and Celtic Religions,* 1988, Syracuse University Press, Syracuse

Davies, Wendy, *Celtic Women in the Early Middle Ages,* 1983, in *Images of Women in Antiquity,* Croom Helm, London, p145-66

DIL, *Dictionary of the Irish Language,* 1913, Royal Irish Academy, Dublin

Dillon, Myles, *The Relationship of Mother and Son, of Father and Daughter, and the Law of Inheritance with Regard to Women,* 1936, in *Studies in Early Irish Law* Hodges Figgis & Co, Dublin, p129-79

---------, *The Cycles of the Kings,* 1946, G. Cumberledge, London

---------, *Early Irish Literature,* 1948, University of Chicago Press, Chicago

Dineen, Rev. Patrick S., *Foclóir Gaedhilge agus Béarla,* 1927, Irish Texts Society, Dublin

Doan, James E., *Women and Goddesses in Early Celtic History, Myth and Legend,* 1987, North-eastern University, Boston

---------, *Sovereignty Aspects in the Roles of Women in Medieval Irish and Welsh Society,* 1984, North-eastern University, Boston

Dobbs, Margaret C., *The Battle of Findchorad,* 1923, in *Zeitschrift für Celtische Philologie* 14:395-420

---------, *The Ban-shenchus,* 1930-2, in *Revue Celtique* 47:238-339; 48:161-234; 49:437-489

Donahue, C., *The Valkyries and the Irish War-Goddesses,* 1941, in *Publications of the Modern Language Association of America* 56:1-12

Dudley, D.R., & Webster, G., *The Rebellion of Boudicca,* 1962, Routledge & Kegan Paul, London

Dumézil, Georges, *Le trio de Macha,* 1954, in *Revue de l'histoire des religions* 146:5-17

Dunn, Vincent A., *Cattle Raids and Courtships: Medieval Narrative Genres in a Traditional Context,* 1989, in *Garland Monographs in Medieval Literature 2,* Garland, London

Duvau, Louis, *La Legende de la Conception de Cuchulainn,* 1888, in *Revue Celtique* 29:1-13

Edwards, Gillian, *Hobgoblin and Sweet Puck: Fairy Names and Natures,* 1974, Geoffrey Bles, London

Ellis, Peter Berresford, *Chronicles of the Celts,* 1999, Robinson, London

Epstein, Angelique G., *War Goddess: The Morrígan and her Germano-Celtic Counterparts,* 1998, UCLA

---------, *Divine Devouring: Further Notes on the Morrígan and the Valkyries,* 1998, in *Journal of Indo-European Studies Monograph* 27:86-104

---------, *The Morrígan and the Valkyries,* 1997, in *Journal of Indo-European Studies Monograph* 21:119-50

---------, *Woman's Words: Threats and Prophecies, Lies and Revelations in Arthurian Romance and Medieval Irish Literature,* 1992, in *Proceedings of the Harvard Celtic Colloquium* 12:184-195

Espérandieu, E., *Recueil General des Bas-Reliefs, Statues et Bustes de la Gaule Romaine,* 1907, Paris

Evans, D. Ellis, *Irish Folk Ways,* 1957, Routledge & Kegan Paul, London

Evans, George Ewart, & Thomson, David, *The Leaping Hare*, 1972, Faber & Faber Ltd, London

Evans, J. Gwenogvryn, *Report on Manuscripts in the Welsh Language*, Volume 1 Part 2 – Peniarth, 1899, Stationery Office, London

Fee, Christopher R., with Leeming, David A., *Gods, Heroes & Kings*, 2001, Oxford University Press, Oxford

Findon, Joanne, *A Woman's Words: Emer and Female Speech in the Ulster Cycle*, 1997, University of Toronto Press, Toronto

Fitzgerald, D., *Popular Tales of Ireland VI: Gearóid Iarla and Áine N'Chliar*, 1879, in *Revue Celtique* 4:185-99

Ford, Patrick K., *Celtic Women: the Opposing Sex*, 1988, in *Viator* 19:417-38

Fraser, J. (ed, trans), *The First Battle of Moytura*, 1916, in *Ériu* 8:1-63

Freeman, Philip Mitchell, *The earliest classical sources on the Celts: A linguistic and historical study*, 1994, Dissertation, Harvard

Fries, Maureen, *Shape-shifting Women in the Old Irish Sagas*, 1991, in *Bestia: Yearbook of the Beast Fable Society*, 3:15-21

Gerald of Wales, *The History and Topography of Ireland*, 1982, Penguin, London

Gibson, H.N., *Status of the Offspring of the Human-Fairy Marriage*, 1953, in *Folklore* 64:282-5

Goedheer, A.J., *Irish and Norse Traditions about the Battle of Clontarf*, 1938, Haarlem

Gower, John, *de confessione amantis*, 1532, Thomas Berthelette, London

Grant, Katherine Whyte, *Myth, Tradition and Story from Western Argyll*, 1925, Oban Times Press, Oban

Gray, Elizabeth A. (ed, trans), *Cath Maige Tuired*, 1982, Irish Texts Society 52

---------, *Cath Maige Tuired: Myth and Structure*, 1982, *Éigse* 19:230-62

Green, Miranda, *The Gods of the Celts*, 1986, Sutton Publishing Ltd, Stroud

Greene, David & O'Connor, Frank, *A Golden Treasury of Irish Poetry AD 600 to 1200*, 1967, Macmillan, London

Gregory, Lady A. (trans), *Cuchulainn of Muirthemne: The Story of the Men of The Red Branch of Ulster*, 1902, John Murray, London

---------, *Irish Myths and Legends*, 1998, Courage Books, Pennsylvania

Gricourt, Jean, *Epona-Rhiannon-Macha*, 1954, in *Ogam* 31:25-40, 137-8; 32:75-86; 34:165-88; 36:269-72

Grinsell, L.V., *Folklore of Prehistoric Sites in Britain*, 1976, Newton Abbot

Guest, Lady Charlotte E., *The Mabinogion*, 1997, Dover Publications Inc., New York

Gwyndaf, Robin, *Welsh Folk Tales*, 1992, National Museum of Wales, Cardiff

Gwynn, Edward (ed, trans), *The Metrical Dindshenchas* (Vol 2), 1906, Royal Irish Academy, Dublin

---------, *The Metrical Dindshenchas* (Vol 3), 1913, Royal Irish Academy, Dublin

---------, *The Metrical Dindshenchas* (Vol 4), 1924, Royal Irish Academy, Dublin

---------, *The Metrical Dindshenchas* (Vol 5), 1935, Royal Irish Academy, Dublin

---------, *On the Idea of Fate in Irish Literature*, 1910, in *Journal of the Ivernian Society* 2:152-65

Hamel, Anton Gerard van, *On Lebor Gabála*, 1915, *Zeitschrift für Celtische Philologie* 10:97-197

Hanley, W., *Tales and Legends of the Banshee*, 1908, in *Ireland's Own XII* no. 312

Henderson, G (ed, trans), *Fled Bricrend, The Feast of Bricriu*, 1899, David Nutt, London

---------, *Survivals in Beliefs among the Celts*, 1911, Glasgow

Hennessy, W.M., *The Ancient Irish Goddess of War*, 1870, in *Revue Celtique* 1:32-55

Henry, P.L., *Verba Scáthaige*, 1990, in *Celtica* 21:191-207

Herbert, Kathleen, *Looking for the Lost Gods of England*, 1994, Anglo-Saxon Books, Norfolk

Herbert, M., *Goddess and King: The Sacred Marriage in Early Ireland*, 1992, in *Women and Sovereignty* (ed L.A. Fradenberg)

---------, *Transmutation of an Irish Goddess*, 1996, in *The Concept of the Goddess*, Routledge, London

Hood, Thomas, *The Works of Thomas Hood, edited by his Son and Daughter* (11 volumes), 1882-4, Ward Lock & Co, London

Hogan, E., *Onomasticon Goedelicum*, 1910, Dublin

Hughes, Ted, *Crow: From the Life and Songs of the Crow*, 1972, Faber & Faber Ltd, London

Hull, Eleanor, *The Cuchullin Saga in Irish Literature*, 1898, David Nutt, London

---------, *Folklore of the British Isles*, 1928, Methuen & Co. Ltd, London

Hull, Vernam, *Ces Ulad*, 1962, in *Zeitschrift für Celtische Philologie* 29:305-14

---------, *Noínden Ulad: The Debility of the Ulidians*, 1968, *Celtica* 8:1-42

Hyde, Douglas, *The Cooking of the Great Queen (Fulacht na Morrigna)*, 1914, in *Celtic Review* 10:335-51

---------, *Báirne Mór*,   1932, in *Béaloideas* 3:187-95

Jackson, Kenneth (ed), *Cath Maighe Léna*, 1938, Dublin Institute for Advanced Studies, Dublin

Jones, Bryan J., *Traditions and Superstitions Collected at Kilcurry, County Louth, Ireland*, 1899, in *Folklore* 10:119-23

Jones, Gwenan, *A Washer at the Ford*, 1922, in *Aberystwyth Studies* 4:105-9

Jonson, Ben, *Selected Works*, 1972, Holt Rinehart & Winston, New York

Keats, John, *John Keats: The Complete Poems*, 1977, Penguin Books, London

Keegan, John, *Legends and Tales of the Queen's County Peasantry*, 1839, in *The Dublin University Magazine* 14:366-74

Kelly, Eamonn P., *Sheela-na-Gigs: Origins and Functions*, 1996, National Museum of Ireland, Dublin

Kinsella, Thomas (trans), *The Tain*, 1970, Oxford University Press, Oxford

Knott, Eleanor (ed),   *Togail Bruidne Da Derga*, 1936, Dublin Institute for Advanced Studies, Dublin

Knott, Eleanor & Murphy, Gerard, *Early Irish Literature*, 1966, Barnes & Noble Inc, New York

Lejeune, M. & Marichal, R., *Textes gaulois et gallo-romains en cursive latine, II: Chamalières*, 1976-77, in *Études Celtiques* 15:151-68

LeMen, R.F., *Traditions et Superstitions de la Basse-Bretagne*, 1870, In *Revue Celtique* 1:225-242, 414-435

LeRoux, Francoise,   *La Mort de Cúchulainn. Commentaire du texte*,
    1966, in *Revue Celtique* 1:225-42, 414-35
---------, *Morrígan-Bodb-Macha, la souveraineté guerrière de l'Irelande*, 1983,
    in *Celticum* 25
Loomis, Roger S., *Morgan le Fee and Celtic Goddesses*, 1940, in *Speculum*
    20:183-203
---------, *Celtic Myth and Arthurian Romance*, 1926, Columbia University
    Press, New York
Lottner, C., *Response to Hennessy, "The Ancient Irish Goddess of War"*,
    1870, in *Revue Celtique* 1:55-57
Lucas, A.T., *Cattle in Ancient Ireland*, 1989, Boethius Press, Kilkenny
Lysaght, Patricia, *The Banshee: The Irish Death Messenger*, 1986, Roberts
    Rinehart Publishers, Colorado
---------, *Aspects of the Earth-Goddess in Traditions of the Banshee*, 1996, in
    The Concept of the Goddess, Routledge, London
MacAlister, R.A. Stewart (ed, trans), *Lebor Gabála Érenn: The Book of the
    Taking of Ireland* (Volume 3), 1940, Irish Texts Society, London
---------, *Lebor Gabála Érenn: The Book of the Taking of Ireland* (Volume 4),
    1941, Irish Texts Society, London
---------, *Lebor Gabála Érenn: The Book of the Taking of Ireland* (Volume 5),
1956, Irish Texts Society, London
MacCana, Proinsias, *Aspects of the Theme of King and Goddess in Irish
    Literature*, 1955-59, in *Études Celtiques* 7:76-114, 356-413; 8:59-65
---------, *Celtic Mythology*, 1970, Hamlyn, London
---------, *Laíded, Gressacht*, 1992, in *Ériu* 43:69-92
MacCulloch, J.A., *The Mythology of All Races* , 1918, in *Celtica* 3:30.
MacKenzie, Donald A., *Scottish Folk Lore and Folk Life*, 1935, Blackie,
    London
Mackinnon, D., *Fulacht na Morrígna*, 1912, in *The Celtic Review* 8:74-6
MacLeod, Fiona, *The Washer at the Ford: and other Legendary Moralities*,
    1896, The Celtic Library, Edinburgh
MacNiocaill, Gearóid, *Ireland before the Vikings*, 1972, Gill, Dublin
MacPhail, Malcolm,   *A bhean nighe*, 1898, in *Folklore* 9:91-2
Magrath, John Mac Rory, *Caithréimm Thoirdhealbhaigh (The Triumphs of
    Turlough)*, 1929, Simpkin Marshall Limited, London
Mallory, J.P. (ed), *Aspects of the Táin*, 1992, December Publications, Belfast
Malory, Sir Thomas, *Le Morte D'Arthur*, 1996, Wordsworth Editions Ltd,
    Hertfordshire
Mancoff, Debra (ed), *The Arthurian Revival: Essays on Form, Tradition, and
    Transformation*, 1992, Garland Publishing Inc., London
Marcellus, Ammianus, *Roman History*, 1940, William Heinemann, London
Marstrander, Carl, *A New Version of the Battle of Mag Rath*, 1911, in *Ériu*
    5:226-47
McAnally, D.R., *Irish Wonders*, 1888, London
McGrath, Sheena, *The Sun Goddess: Myth, Legend and History*, 1997,
    Blandford, London
Mee, Arthur, *Leicestershire and Rutland*, 1937, Hodder & Stoughton, London
Meyer, Kuno, (ed, trans) *Cáin Adamnán*,   1905, Clarendon Press, Oxford

----------, *The Wooing of Emer*, 1888, in *The Archaeological Review* 1:68-75, 151-55, 231-35, 298-307

----------, *The Oldest Version of Tochmarc Emire*, 1890, in *Revue Celtique* 11:424-55

----------, *Sanas Cormaic: An Old-Irish Glossary*, 1912, Hodges Figgis & Co Ltd, Dublin

Miller, Arthur W.K. (ed), *O'Clery's Irish Glossary*, 1879-83, in *Revue Celtique* 4:349-428; 5:1-69

Miller, Hugh, *Scenes and Legends of the North of Scotland*, 1835, A & C Black, Edinburgh

Murphy, Gerard, *Notes on Cath Maige Tuired*, 1956, *Éigse* 8:191-98

Murray, James A.H., *Thomas of Erceldoune*, 1875, N. Trübner & Co, London

Nettlau, Max, *The Fragment of the Táin Bó Cúailnge in MSS Egerton 93*, 1894, in *Revue Celtique* 15:62-78, 198-208

Ní Bhrolcháin, M., *Women in Early Irish Myths and Sagas*, 1980, in *The Crane Bag* 4:1, 12-19

Ní Dhonnchadha, M., *Caillech and Other Terms for Veiled Women in Medieval Irish Texts*, 1994, in *Éigse* 28:71-96

Ní Dhuibhne, E., *The Old Woman as Hare: Structure and Meaning in an Irish Legend*, 1993, in *Folklore* 104:77-85

Nildin-Wall, Bodil, *The Witch as Hare or the Witch's Hare: Popular Legends and Beliefs in Nordic Tradition*, 1993, in *Folklore* 104:67-76

Ó Broin, T. (ed), *Scéaltaí Tíre: Bailiúchán Seanchais ó Ghaillimh*, 1957, Baile Átha, Cliath

----------, *What is the "Debility of the Ulstermen"?*, 1963, in *Éigse* 10:286-99

Ó Cathasaigh, T., *The Semantics of "Síd"*, 1977, in *Éigse* 17:137-55

Ó Cuív, Brian (ed), *Cath Muighe Tuireadh*, 1945, Dublin Institute for Advanced Studies, Dublin

----------, *The Romance of Mis and Dubh Ruis*, 1952, in *Celtica* 2:325-33

O Curry, Eugene, *On the Manners and Customs of the Ancient Irish*, 1873, Williams and Norgate, London

O Donovan, John (ed), *The Banquet of Dun na n-Gedh and The Battle of Magh Rath*, 1842, Irish Archaeological Society, Dublin

----------, *Supplement to O'Reilly's Irish-English Dictionary*, 1864, James Duffy & Co, Dublin

----------, *Sanas Chormaic: Cormac's Glossary*, 1868, Whitley Stokes, Dublin

O'Grady, S.H., *Silva Gadelica*, 1892, London

O'Grady, Standish, *The Triumph and Passing of Cú Chulainn*, 1920, The Talbot Press, Dublin

----------, *Caithréim Thoirdhealbhaigh*, 1929, Irish Texts Society, London

Ó hÓgáin, D., *Gearóid Iarla agus an Dratíocht*, 1977, in *Scríobh 4:234-59*

O'Leary, Philip, *The Honour of Women in Early Irish Literature*, 1987, in *Ériu* 38:27-44

Olmsted, Garrett S., *The Gods of the Celts and the Indo-Europeans*, 1994, Archaeolingua, Budapest

O'Rahilly. Cecile (ed), *The Stowe Version of the Táin Bó Cúailnge*, 1961, Dublin Institute for Advanced Studies, Dublin

----------, (ed), *Táin Bó Cúailnge from the Book of Leinster*, 1967, Dublin Institute for Advanced Studies,\ Dublin

---------, (ed), *Táin Bó Cúailnge Recension I*, 1976, Dublin Institute for Advanced Studies, Dublin

O'Rahilly, Thomas F., *Early Irish History and Mythology*, 1946, Dublin Institute for Advanced Studies, Dublin

---------, *Irish Dialects*, 1976, Dublin

Ó Riain, Pádraig (ed), *Cath Almaine*, 1978, Dublin Institute for Advanced Studies, Dublin

Ó Súilleabháin, S., *A Handbook of Irish Folklore*, 1942, Dublin

d'Outremeuse, Jean, *Ly Myreur des Histors. Fragment du Second Livres (Annees 794-826)*, 1965, Broché, Brussels

Pálsson, Hermann & Fox, Denton, *Grettir's Saga*, 1974, Toronto

Paton, Lucy, *Studies in the Fairy Mythology of Arthurian Romance*, 1903, Ginn & Co, Boston

Petrie, George, *On the History and Antiquities of Tara Hill*, 1939, Dublin

Pokorny, Julius, *Indogermanisches Etymologisches Wörterbuch* (IEW), 1959, Munich, 2 volumes

Pollington, Stephen, *Leechcraft: Early English Charms, Plant Lore and Healing*, 2000, Anglo-Saxon Books, Norfolk

Radner, Joan N. (ed, trans), *Fragmentary Annals of Ireland*, 1978, Dublin Institute for Advanced Studies, Dublin

Rankin, H.D., *Celts and the Classical World*, 1987, Croom Helm, London

Rees, Alwyn & Brinley, *Celtic Heritage: Ancient Tradition in Ireland and Wales*, 1961, Thames & Hudson, New York

Renard, M., *Poteries a Masques Prophylactiques*, 1955, in *Latomus* 14:202-40

Rhys, John, *Celtic Folk-Lore, Welsh and Manx* (2 volumes), 1901, Oxford University Press, Oxford

Ritson, Joseph, *A Dissertation on Fairies*, 1831, London

Rolleston, T.W., *Myths and Legends of the Celtic Race*, 1911, G.G. Harrap & Co, London

Ross, Anne, *Pagan Celtic Britain*, 1967, Thames & Hudson, London

---------, *The Divine Hag of the Pagan Celts*, in *The Witch Figure*, Venetia Newell (ed), 1973, Routledge & Kegan Paul, London

---------, *The Folklore of the Scottish Highlands*, 1976, B.T. Batsford, London

---------, *Folklore of Wales*, 2001, Tempus Publishing Ltd, Stroud

Royal Irish Academy, *Dictionary of the Irish Language* (DIL), 1983, Dublin University Press, Dublin

Russell, Paul, *The Sounds of a Silence: The Growth of Cormac's Glossary*, 1988, in *Cambridge Medieval Celtic Studies* 15:1-30

Sayers, W., *Airdrech, Sirite and Other Early Irish Battlefield Spirits*, 1991, in *Éigse* 25:45-55

Schlauch, Margaret (trans), *The Saga of the Volsungs, the Saga of Ragnar Lodbrok, Together with the Lay of Kraka*, 1930, W.W. Norton & Co, New York

Schoepperle, Gertrude, *The Washer at the Ford*, 1919, in *The Journal of English and Germanic Philology* 18:60-6

Scott, Sir Walter, *Minstrelsy of the Scottish Border*, 1802, Edinburgh

---------, *Letters on Demonology and Witchcraft*, 1831, London

Scowcroft, R. Mark, *Leabhar Gabhála Part I: The Growth of the Text*, 1987, in *Ériu* 38:81-142

---------, *Leabhar Gabhála Part II: The Growth of the Tradition*, 1988, in *Ériu* 39:1-66

Sébillot, Paul, *Le Folk-lore de France*, 1905, Paris: Librairie orientale et americaine

Shelley, Percy Blythe, *The Works of P.B. Shelley*, 1994, Wordsworth Editions Ltd, Hertfordshire

Siculus, Diodorus, *The Library of History*, 1933, William Heinemann, London

Sikes, Wirt, *British Goblins: Welsh Folklore, Fairy Mythology, Legends and Traditions*, 1880, S. Low Marston Searle & Rivington, London

Silius, Italicus, *Punica*, 1934, William Heinemann, London

Simms, Katherine, *Women in Norman Ireland*, 1978, in *Women in Irish Society: The Historical Dimension*, Dublin, p14-25

Spenser, Edmund, *The Faery Queen*, 1901, Frederick Warne & Co, London

Statius, Publius Papinus, *Statius*, 1928, William Heinemann, London

Stedman, Edmund (ed), *A Victorian Anthology 1837-1895*, 1895, MacMillan & Co, London

St. John, Charles, *Short Sketches of the Wild Sports and Natural History of the Highlands*, 1846, London

Stock, Lorraine K., *The Hag of Castle Hautdesert: The Celtic Sheela-na-gig and the Auncian in Sir Gawain and the Green Knight*, 2001, in *On Arthurian Women*, Scriptorium Press, Dallas

Stokes, Whitley (ed), *Three Irish Glosses*, 1862, Williams & Norgate, London

---------, (trans), *Cuchulainn's Death, Abridged from the Book of Leinster*, 1876, in *Revue Celtique* 3:175-85

---------, (ed, trans), *On the Metrical Glossaries of the Medieval Irish*, 1891, in *Transactions of the Philological Society* p1-103

---------, (ed, trans), *The Bodleian Dinnshenchas*, 1892, in *Folklore* 3:467-516

---------, *The Edinburgh Dinnshenchas*, 1893, in *Folklore* 4:471-97

---------, (ed, trans), *The Prose Tales in the Rennes Dinnshenchas*, 1894-5, in *Revue Celtique* 15:273-484; 16:30-167, 269-312

---------, (ed), *O'Mulconry's Glossary*, 1899, in *Archiv für Celtische Lexikographie* 1:232-323, 473-481

---------, (ed, trans), *Bruiden Da Chocae, Da Choca's Hostel*, 1900, in *Revue Celtique* 21:149-65, 312-27. 388-402

---------, (ed), *The Lecan Glossary*, 1900, in *Archiv für Celtische Lexikographie* 1:50-100

---------, (ed, trans), *The Destruction of Dá Derga's Hostel*, 1901, in *Revue Celtique* 22:9-61, 165-215, 282-329, 390-437

---------, (ed, trans), *The Death of Crimthann Son of Fidach, and the Adventures of the Sons of Eochaid Muigmedón*, 1903, in *Revue Celtique* 24:172-207

---------, (ed), *O'Davoren's Glossary*, 1904, in *Archiv für Celtische Lexikographie* 2:197-231, 339-503

---------, (ed), *The Glossary in Egerton 158*, 1906, in *Archiv für Celtische Lexikographie* 3:145-214, 247-8

---------, (ed), *The Stowe Glossaries*, 1907, in *Archiv für Celtische Lexikographie* 3:268-89

--------, (ed, trans), *The Training of Cúchulainn,* 1908, in *Revue Celtique* 29:109-52

Sutherland, Dr Arthur, *The Venomous Wild Boar of Glen Glass,* 1892, in *The Highland Monthly* 4:491, Inverness

Tacitus, Cornelius, *Germania,* 1914, William Heinemann, London

--------, *The Histories,* 1925, William Heinemann, London

--------, *The Annals,* 1925, William Heinemann, London

Taylor, Thomas (trans), *Life of St. Samson of Dol,* 1925, SPCK, London

Thomas, J.W. (trans), *The Crown: A Tale of Sir Gawain and King Arthur's Court by Heinrich von dem Türlin,* 1989, University of Nebraska Press, Lincoln

Todd, J.H. (ed), *Cogadh Gaedhel re Gallaibh,* 1867, London

Tongue, R.L., *Forgotten Folk-Tales of the English Counties,* 1970, Routledge & Kegan Paul, London

Topsell, Edward, *The Historie of Four-Footed Beastes,* 1607, William Taggard, London

de Troyes, Chrétien, *Le Chevalier au Lion,* 1960, Champion, Paris

--------, *Erec et Enide,* 1952, Champion, Paris

Tymoczko, Maria (trans), *Two Death Tales from the Ulster Cycle: The Death of Cu Roi and the Death of Cu Chulainn,* 1981, Dolmen Press, Dublin

Watson, E.C., *Highland Mythology,* 1908, in *The Celtic Review* 5:48-70

Weir, Anthony, *Images of Lust: Sexual Carvings on Medieval Churches,* 1986, B.T. Batsford Ltd, London

Wemple, Suzanne F., *Sanctity and Power: The Dual Pursuit of Early Medieval Women,* in *Becoming Visible: Women in European History,* 1977, Houghton Mifflin, Boston

Westwood, Kate, *Black Annis – Leicester Legend or Widespread Myths?,* 1998, White Dragon Magazine, Samhain issue

Wheeler, Bonnie & Tolhurst, Fiona (eds), *On Arthurian Women,* 2001, Scriptorium Press, Dallas

Wilhelm, James J. (ed), *The Romance of Arthur: an Anthology of Medieval Texts in Translation,* 1994, Garland Publishing, New York

Williams, J.E. Caerwyn, & Ford, Patrick K., *The Irish Literary Tradition,* 1992, University of Wales Press, Cardiff

Wood-Martin, W.G., *Traces of the Elder Faiths of Ireland,* 1902, Longmans Green & Co, London

Yeats, W.B., *Fairy and Folk Tales of Ireland,* 1983, MacMillan, London

Index

195

197

flesh, *26, 32, 48, 51, 125, 146, 161, 183, 184*

flint, *180*

Florent, *92*

foal, *72, 158*

Fogartach, *113*

Fomorian, *10, 12, 14, 15, 31*

Fomorians, *10, 14, 15, 31, 35, 122*

food, *15, 26, 64, 89, 172, 183*

ford, *14, 18, 23, 60, 84, 100, 108, 110, 116, 120, 121, 141, 147*

Ford of Barking, *168*

Ford of Unshin, *14*

fords, *65, 73, 158, 171*

Forgall, *19, 173*

Forgall Monach, *19*

forked staff, *21*

foster mother, *148*

foster-mothers, *12, 106*

Fotla, *40, 54, 94, 95, 154, 156*

Founding of Emain Macha, *97*

four, *182*

four nights, *38, 104, 108*

France, *65, 120, 134, 135, 150, 152, 177*

François Bader, *148*

French, *35, 98, 133, 177*

Frenzy, *40*

fruit, *79*

Fuath, *73, 117, 158, 170*

fúir, *34*

Fury, *33, 34, 40*

Gae Bolga, *20, 23, 24, 173*

Gaheris, *132*

Gallic, *83, 147, 150, 152, 167, 171*

gan, *128*

Garech, *52*

Gareth, *132*

gargoyles, *178*

Gaul, *150, 152*

Gauls, *129*

Gawain, *90, 132, 133, 178*

geese, *152*

geis, *26, 27, 82, 86, 87, 104, 105, 159*

genitalia, *177, 178*

Gentle Annie, *45, 63, 146*

Geoffrey of Monmouth, *128, 132*

ges, *105*

gessa, *105*

giant, *49, 64, 103, 132*

gigantic, *39, 103*

Gilgamesh, *18*

Glaistig, *72, 73, 158*

Glastigs, *73, 158*

Glen Glass, *80, 137, 149, 159, 164*

Glenn na mbodhar, *25*

Gliten, *129*

Gliton, *129*

Glitonea, *129*

glossary, *32*

glossopetrae, *180*

goats, *44, 46*

God of Battle, *30, 34, 52, 97, 142*

God of Light, *20*

Goddess, *8, 12, 18, 20, 22, 24, 26, 30, 31, 33, 34, 37, 38, 41, 42, 48, 49, 50, 51, 52, 54, 55, 57, 59, 60, 65, 83, 85, 86, 87, 89, 96, 97, 98, 100, 106, 109, 112, 115, 122, 127, 128, 129, 132, 133, 134, 136, 137, 139, 140, 142, 143, 147, 148, 149, 150, 151, 152, 153, 159, 161, 166, 167, 168, 171, 172, 173, 182*

Goddess of Fate, *109, 122*

Goddess of the Land, *33*

Goddess of the Waters, *33*

Gododdin, *132*

gold, *133, 166*

golden hair, *73, 75, 114, 140, 158*

goose, *152, 153*

gorse, *44*

Gort na Morrígna, *61*

Govannon, *151*

Grainne, *48, 59, 149, 159, 164*

Great Queen, *33, 85, 172*

Greek myth, *125*

Greek myths, *10*

green, *47, 72, 73, 79, 116, 132, 133, 141, 158*

Green Knight, *90, 132, 133, 177*

gressacht, *19*

Grettir's Saga, *18*

grey, *154*

Grian, *80*

201

202

203

OTHER BOOKS BY THESE AUTHORS

ARTEMIS
Virgin Goddess of the Sun & Moon
Sorita D'Este
Avalonia, 2005 – ISBN 1-905297-02-5

Climbing The Tree of Life
A Manual for Exploring the Magickal Qabalah
David Rankine
Avalonia, 2005 – ISBN 1-905297-01-7

Becoming Magick
New & Revised Magicks for the New Aeon
David Rankine
Mandrake of Oxford, 2004 – ISBN 1-869928-81-4

The Practical Angel Magic of Dr. John Dee's Enochian Tables
Tabula Bonorum Angelorum Invocationes
Stephen Skinner & David Rankine
Golden Hoard Press, 2004 – ISBN 0-954763-90-4

Crystals – Healing & Folklore
The uses and symbolism of crystals in folklore, myths and religion
David Rankine
Capall Bann Publishing, 2002 - ISBN 1-861632-00-2

Printed in the United States
3928LVS00002B/151